7/105B
4/14/SC
4/17 dk

22240593

Indigo and Other Poems

This edition is limited to
five hundred numbered copies,
of which this is Number *3 2*

For Carl,
Whose Prisoners of the Good Fight
moved me deeply. May we meet again.
Salud!
Amron
1-18-91

Also by Aaron Kramer

Poetry

Another Fountain
Till the Grass is Ripe for Dancing
Thru Our Guns
The Glass Mountain
The Thunder of the Grass
The Golden Trumpet
Thru Every Window!
Denmark Vesey
Roll the Forbidden Drums!
The Tune of the Calliope
Moses
Rumshinsky's Hat
Henry at the Grating
On the Way to Palermo
O Golden Land!
Carousel Parkway
In Wicked Times
The Burning Bush
In the Suburbs

Translation

The Poetry and Prose of Heinrich Heine
Morris Rosenfeld: The Teardrop Millionaire
Goethe, Schiller, Heine: Songs and Ballads
Rilke: Visions of Christ
The Emperor of Atlantis

Criticism

The Prophetic Tradition in American Poetry: 1835–1900
Melville's Poetry: Toward the Enlarged Heart

Contributions to Symposia

Seven Poets in Search of an Answer
Poetry Therapy
Poetry the Healer
Paumanok Rising
Life Guidance Through Literature

Anthologies

On Freedom's Side
A Century of Yiddish Poetry

Indigo and Other Poems

Aaron Kramer

With a Foreword by Joseph Wershba
and an Introduction by Richard E. Braun

Cornwall Books
New York • London • Toronto

Cornwall Books
440 Forsgate Drive
Cranbury, NJ 08512

Cornwall Books
25 Sicilian Avenue
London WC1A 2QH, England

Cornwall Books
P.O. Box 39, Clarkson Pstl. Stn.
Mississauga, Ontario,
L5J 3X9 Canada

The paper used in this publication meets the requirements of the American National Standard for Permanence of Paper for Printed Library Materials Z39.48-1984.

for Kitty

Library of Congress Cataloging-in-Publication Data

Kramer, Aaron, 1921–
    Indigo and other poems / Aaron Kramer ; with a foreword by Joseph Wershba and an introduction by Richard E. Braun.
        p.   cm.
    ISBN 0-8453-4828-0 (alk. paper)
    I. Title.
PS3521.R29I54   1991
811'.52—dc20   90-55061
                                                                                    CIP

PRINTED IN THE UNITED STATES OF AMERICA

Contents

Acknowledgments

First of all to Richard E. Braun, distinguished University of Alberta professor, poet, and editor of *Modern Poetry Studies*, who read this manuscript with great care and sensitivity. His advice has strengthened the collection considerably.

Acknowledgment is also given to the following journals in which many of these poems have appeared: *American Man*, for "Job Interview" and "The Slippers"; *Antigonish Review*, for "Raking"; *Bitter-root*, for "Dental Appointment: 3," "Hero," and "Wives"; *Black Buzzard Review*, for "Outside Penn Station"; *Brooklyn College Literary Review*, for "At Trudie's Trivia Door," "Dental Appointment: 6," "Nick," and "Object Seen from Moving Window"; *California Quarterly*, for "Granada: First Showing" and "How California Was"; *Confrontation*, for "Dental Appointment: 1, 4, 5," "Nightsongs: 2," and "Southshore Line"; *Cumberland Poetry Journal*, for "Flood," "Grins," "Visiting Hours are Over: 3," "What Comes Home," "Without a Camera," and "Yawn in Empty House"; *Earthwise*, for "Words"; *Eleven*, for "Anniversary Waltz"; *Free Lance*, for "The Tourist"; *Freedomways*, for "For Benjamin Moloise"; *Icarus*, for "Penguintown: TV Special" and "The Word"; *Jewish Currents*, for "The Next Wave"; *Journal of Humanistic Psychology*, for "Anniversary" and "Postoperative Care"; *Journal of Poetry Therapy*, for "Going In: 3"; *Kenyon Review*, for "Blizzard," "Homecoming," "Passengers," and "Reflections"; *Lodestar*, for "Cheerleader Killed; 'Best Student' Seized" and "Rhodos"; *Long Pond Review*, for "Street Scene"; *Lyric*, for "April," "Granddaughters: 1," "Incident," and "Nightsongs: 1, 3"; *Lyrismos*, for "Air for Bagpipe"; *Mickle Street Review*, for "Legacy"; *Midstream*, for "Grandmother"; *Modern Poetry Studies*, for "Fire," "Pastoral," and "Tree"; *New England Review*, for "Episode: 1, 3, 4," "In the Suburbs," "Indigo," "Local," "Neighbors," "New York Skyline in Cloud," "Old Tunes," and "Trout Quintet"; *North Atlantic Review*, for "Barcelona: the Last Night," "The Little Swiss Sheepgirl," and "Time Machine"; *Piedmont Literary Review*, for "Reunion: She allowed my invitation"; *Pikestaff Forum,* for "Night Thoughts"; *Poet Lore,* for "Parking Lot" and "Scarf"; *Prairie Wind,* for "Canadian Geese," "Going In: 1," and "Greg Norman's Five-Wood"; *Riverrun,* for "Lip on Lip," "Morning Stroll After Hurricane," and "Wake"; *San Fernando Poetry Journal,* for "In the Fortieth Presidency: 1, 2," "Learning by Stages," and "The Masters of Düsseldorf"; *South & West,* for "A New Year"; *Spectrum,* for "Eva!"; *Street,* for "Mycenae: On Brushing One's Shoes in Athens" and "O Minos! O Rhadamanthys!"; *Sun Dog,* for "One Year the Leaves Were Late"; *Sycamore Review,* for "Centennial: 'Live from the Met'"; *Transitions,* for "Toward the End"; *Visions,* for "Had I Not," "In the Fortieth Presidency: 3," "Port Jefferson: A November Day," and "The Voice of San Miguel"; and *Wind,* for "Blue Square," "Episode: 2, 5," "Going In: 4," "Granddaughters: 2," "News Item," "Storm," and "Windchimes."

In addition, some of these poems have appeared in anthologies, as follows: "The Cliché," in *Anthology of Magazine Verse,* 1984; "Birthday," in *Anthology of Magazine Verse, 1985;* "Charlie," in *Anthology of Magazine Verse, 1989;* "Interview," in *The Bloom;* "Dialog," in *Discover America;* "Several Miles Apart," in *Friendship Bridge;* "Midnight in Oakdale," in *Island Light;* "The Death of a Friend," in *Life and Love;* "At Night," in *On Good Ground;* "The New Home," in *Paumanok Rising;* "On the Death of Someone Else's Grandchild," in *Poetry Project Four;* "In the Fortieth Presidency: 5," in *Snow Summits;* and "The Son," in *Writers' Forum.*

A few of these poems were first collected in the chapbooks *In Wicked Times* and *In the Suburbs.*

Foreword

Joseph Wershba

Aaron Kramer is nearing his allotted three score and ten (with at least another ten-year bonus in store by reason of his good works). This book of poems covering his sixties bears testament that Kramer is in his mental prime and at the height of his poetic power.

After a lifetime of making poems, Kramer is more surefooted than ever. His poems may be less fleshy with the fatted hopes of bygone years, but they are more muscular and truer in their artist's eye—and, more important, their artist's heart. His subject is simple humanity with a small "h"; thus, he is no stranger to the tragic element that all flesh is heir to.

But there is no useless heat here.

He sits in Penn Station and

> . . . grimly
> examines (once an uplifting, favorite
> pastime) faces of sisters, of brothers
> —no longer with awe, but at least with compassion;
> never, please, never with contempt!

—Compassion, never contempt!

There is your key to the leitmotif of Aaron Kramer's lifetime work.

And where does this abjuration appear? In a "voyage" from the suburbs to the city—for a cringing appointment . . . with the dentist!

Shades of Homer's Ulysses!

How do you make a poem about a toothache and turn it into an overpowering evocation of past struggles for bread and peace in the Union Square demonstrations of the 1930s? How do you make a relatively brief poem that contains all the elemental force of a short novel by Dreiser? How do you make *poems* about applying for a job, moving into a new house in the suburbs, riding home on the commuter LIRR? How do you transform Alzheimer's disease into a symphonic elegy to an eighty-nine-year-old uncle? How do you make poetry about your father crawling home during the Depression with the one or two dollars he made that day selling ties? That is the word Kramer uses: *crawling,* and in that word is all the torment of the mind o'erthrown by forces beyond control, the humiliation of standing in line with three hundred other spirit-broken men searching for the ten-dollar-a-week job that will keep a family fed and united.

How do you make poems about ordinary people in ordinary life and invest them with the music of the Schubert *Trout Quintet?*

You do it Aaron Kramer's way—with compassion, never contempt.

How do you suffuse all the familiarities of suburban living with words that *become music on the page*—and this is done without hearing the poet's reading? Read Kramer aloud in your own voice, and you will see how you can make instant music too about getting up in the morning, having breakfast, going to the job, dealing with an illness in the family, feeling alienated, making a living—all the commonplaces that the poets of our youth steered clear of as "improper" materials for poems.

Aaron Kramer has done all this—admirably. This is poetry of the first order.

It reminds me of a talk years ago with Carl Sandburg about the "cerebral poets" whom the "official" literary judges had established as the final word.

"They wouldn't write a poem for the 'common herd,'" Sandburg snorted. "A poem about democracy? No-o-o. What they want is high, intellectual windings—they're the only ones who know what they're talking about. They are latitudinous and sepulchral," Sandburg chuckled. "They ain't never had no fun. Their stuff comes in wrapped in cellophane—hasn't known the touch of human hands!"

Aaron Kramer's poems are the stuff of human hands. There is the remembrance of a nine-year-old in public school taken in adoration of his "Swiss sheepgirl," turned aside by unfeeling teachers.

Much later, there is the vacation in Greece, remembered with all the resonances of a Byron enamoured of antiquity. And there is the passionate voyage to Spain, almost forty years after Franco

[16]

and his Fascist allies crushed the Republic and opened the way for Hitler's conquest of Europe.

And yes, inevitably, there *is* contempt and disdain—for the aggressor and the oppressor—delivered with an economy of language that makes the curse all the more effective: disdain for the professors at the University of Düsseldorf who split almost evenly against naming their university for Düsseldorf's most famous native lad—Heinrich Heine, the same Heine whose poems were the bread of life for a young Aaron Kramer, and whom Kramer repaid in part in later years by translating his works. There is contempt and disdain for military people and their civilian controllers who play with gadgets like neutron bombs; for presidents who witlessly place wreaths in Bitburg cemetery where Hitler's storm troopers lie buried.

The Holocaust is still too large a subject for most treatment, but in a few deft lines drenched in tears and blood, Kramer calls for God's judgment on the oppressors, in the six lines of "Rendezvous in Hell." There is controlled passion in these brief poems—and it is this control and brevity that raise commentary to the level of art.

Of course it's easier to write poetically and passionately about the dramatic, the heroic, the exotic, than it is to write about the commonplace and ordinary. But Kramer's skill and wide-ranging humanness form the basis for his poetic triumph.

In an age when we have less reason to be optimistic than ever before in history, Kramer still has Whitman coursing through his blood, the Whitman of beauty found in the everydayness of life. Kramer still sees life as struggling and seeking, much as Sandburg saw it—"the people will live on, the learning and blundering people will live on . . . the people, yes"—and always with a respect for human personality, always with the hope for a decent life. For who can live without hope? Kramer still hears the Schubert "Trout" running through his master Heine's lines, and it is this saving serenity that helps keep him sane in an insane world, a world that Churchill has aptly dubbed The Terrible Twentieth Century.

Has Kramer been tempted by the luxury of despair? Does he long at times to muck about in the slough of despond? Has he never turned cynic and retreated behind the shibboleth of What's-the-use, life-is-a-bitch-and-then-you-die, or just as you die you say: Hey, what was *that* about? Kramer is human; he does not confuse constancy with heroics. Of course he grows tired of exhortations to keep up the "good fight." He admits it candidly in

"Dialog," in which the Muse of Politics shakes Kramer awake on 4 July 1976, the two hundredth anniversary of the Declaration of Independence. For crying out loud, boy, says the Muse, the country's lost the spirit of '76 and is going to hell in a handbasket at home and abroad, and why aren't you out there shouting alarums? And Kramer says, Hey Muse, I'm tired; go find another poet, a *younger* poet, to pick up the flag, and let *him* knock *his* head against the wall:

> Go tell him, Muse, America's forgotten
> glories! Let his unpleasant rhymes that once
> roared through my jaws, set her again afire!

Well, every poet is entitled to a day off. But Aaron Kramer, the laughing-eyed, sad and sweet-faced lad I knew more than fifty years ago at Abraham Lincoln High School in Brooklyn, is still aflame.

You can look it up.

It's all in this book.

[18]

Introduction

Richard E. Braun

Judgments

For two decades, I have envisioned a beautiful book. I call it "Collected Poems of Aaron Kramer." It is really a select gathering modeled from Robert Graves' successive editions, which retained a uniform length, however much the writer's total output grew. Such a meticulous picking-process is needed in the case of highly-productive authors. Short poems—the specialty of Kramer as of Graves—are, like the parts of long poems and the episodes of drama, improvisations: as such, they must be subject to after-thought, with attendant acceptance, alteration, or excision.

But, while Graves was a stern critic who castigated himself as harshly as he did others, Kramer is a man who accepts the formulation Dylan Thomas made in his "Note" to the 1953 *Collected Poems:*

> Some of them I have revised a little, but if I went on revising everything that I now do not like in this book, I should be so busy that I would have no time to try to write new poems.

For Kramer, as for Thomas, creation—that lively renewal of self and world—must never come second to the sometimes pedantic work of emendation. I would speculate that, in both men, this odd combination of pride and humility is one sign of genius. The consequence, however, for Kramer's imagined "Collected Poems"—I have long felt—will be that another man than he must do the censorial task of selecting. If that agent succeeds, the product should vindicate Kramer's half century of effort with permanence.

As I write this, the contents and arrangement of *Indigo* are not settled. My manuscript seems to be missing a few poems. The publisher is now copyediting; the poet, revising. Even so, I can say that *Indigo* is a positive contribution to the Kramerian corpus. And, despite doubt concerning the book's final form, I will attempt to identify the pieces that I think merit a place in the long longed-for Select Collection, and to list them in provisional order of appearance. In so committing myself, I in no way wish to preempt or deter readers who, studying the whole, published volume, will make different choices, and assemble, as we all do, their personal Collections in keeping with their tastes and critical standards.

Now I must stand alone, though, and deliver judgment. I believe that the poems that follow are excellent. Generally, they are very well crafted indeed: the diction fresh, the rhythm pliant and controlled, the ordering of parts apt. As whole structures, I find them not only rationally justifiable, but charming, or intriguing, or able to elicit strong emotion. (He who could read "The Death of a Friend" unmoved is, if not lost beyond redemption, then hardened beyond appeal.) Here, then, is my list:

Indigo	The Tourist	The Son
Visitors	The Word	Learning
Quarrel	O Minos! O	The Little Swiss
Fire	Rhadamanthys!	Sheepgirl
Weeding	At Trudie's Trivia	The Next Wave
Job Interview	Door	Going In
Midnight in	Yawn in Empty	Visiting Hours Are
Oakdale	House	Over
Night Thoughts	Grandmother	Wives
Windchimes	Without a Camera	A New Year
Nightsongs	On the Death of	April
Hero	Someone Else's	Pastoral
Dialog	Grandchild	One Year the
Street Scene	The Death of a	Leaves Were Late
Air for Bagpipe	Friend	Wake
The Yucca	The Face of Rose	
Legacy	Toward the End	

Observations

People commonly expect an author who maintains traditional types—the Flaubertian novel, for example, or the Petrarchan sonnet—also to uphold established ideas and associations. Lovers of artistic literature, of poetry particularly, have brains that buzz with the swarming connotations of all words. But most resonant and constant is the buzzing induced by words, and images, that refer to the civilization's abiding symbols: sacred symbols that act on men's fear, hope, and affection. Many of these loving readers have, I am sure, been puzzled to find that the formal verse of Aaron Kramer has tended to simplify or ignore the powerful and seemingly inescapable connotations of religious references.

This is a problem not for Kramer alone, but for the culture of America and Europe generally. As Mircea Eliade has pointed out (*The Sacred and the Profane*, 1957):

> It is only in the modern societies of the West that nonreligious man has developed fully. Modern nonreligious man assumes a new existential situation; he regards himself solely as the subject and agent of history.

Many moderns have converted the Christ to an ordinary reformer or, like Kramer, have defined His crucified form narrowly as an historical symbol of mankind suffering under tyranny. Similarly, many have preceded Kramer in misusing allusions to ancient Greek and Greco-Roman piety by reducing these vehicles of sacred significance to decorative or illustrative, or merely organizational, functions. Again, to encounter rhyming verse in which the Hebrew Testament's Burning Bush, bereft of the numinous nature of Divinity, has become a metaphor for the vitality of the Jewish nation, would doubtless baffle many poetry readers.

Poetry, in fact, has not often been secular. To compose verse under the influence of the secularism of modern Western society, with its scientistic and socialistic bias, is hard and risky. The risk is that one may say what is not intended, as Kramer did in the poem "Anniversary." There, by using the word "hell" as a purely descriptive word for intolerable pain, he accidentally implies that the torture is deserved; for Hell holds none but the guilty. To employ a lowercase *h* does not remove this inherited meaning, but at most diverts it momentarily to merely expressive use.

Now, as Eliade might have predicted, a change is made in *Indigo* that is in accord with changes in American bourgeois culture. Since the sixties—rather, since that revolutionary "Great Year" of twelve years from 1957 to 1970—institutional religion has accelerated its decline among the middle classes. The Church, more than the Chapel; the Temple, more than the Synagogue, has become, in the idiom of thirty years ago, "increasingly irrelevant." But in the individual, spirituality has had a resurgence.

[21]

This resurgence is, as usual, the outcome of initiation: initiation by upheaval. The initiation was made possible by the survival of the notion of the sanctity of life. That this sanctity should have maintained recognition in secularist times is due to the commendably self-contradicting behavior of modern men like Aaron Kramer, whose voice has always risen in behalf of the victims of ruthless or complacent power.

The initiation was brought about, or at least potentiated, by converging causes: the Civil Rights movement, the psychedelic movement, and reaction against the Vietnam War. The Great Year began with the independence of Ghana; with Little Richard and Elvis Presley; with Sputnik; with Alan Watts and Maharishi Mahesh Yogi. It comprised ordeals of passage through the four elements: earth, as in the tunnels of the Viet Cong; air, as in the space race; and fire versus water, as in Watts, Detroit, and Newark. The year ended with the Kent State massacre and the invocation of the Canadian War Measures Act. Also, it began with Timothy Leary and ended with G. Gordon Liddy.

Today, one faces this paradox: that in the person of American intellectuals like Aaron Kramer, nonreligious, "existential" man is resacralizing himself and his world. This was already evident shortly after the end of the Great Year, when Kramer employed initiatory imagery with brilliance: by fire, in "Fire" (first published in 1971), and by air, fire, then climactically by water in the masterpiece "Mr. Glicklich Takes a Shower" (first published in 1973, reprinted in *Carousel Parkway,* 1980, and *The Burning Bush,* 1983). Today, *Indigo* superbly promotes that metamorphosis from the materialism of disillusion to a spirituality of acute perception.

To begin, see where the poem "Indigo" begins:

> Maybe there is, after all,
> something behind it—
> something that summons me
> out of a deepening blue
> and chooses me to choose. . . .

There is no need, here, to speak the word "God," with its unmanageable cargo of culturally established connotations. The essence of Kramer's new, very new, book is here: in the loving cohesion of family, in the reverence for craft, and in dread at "the death of a stranger."

Love and fear: these are what Kramer expresses best, and now combines with a sense of restored, physical, commonplace sacred-

ness. The grandmother of "Grandmother" must tunnel and fly—
dire ordeal of burial and awesome ascent—to come to where her
dear one

> . . . finds her hand reaching the milk to his mouth,
> her eyes reaching the sparkle to his eyes,
> her lips reaching the love to his belly button.

Terror and love are the field of Kramer's mastery. He an-
nounces this in "A New Year," and profoundly demonstrates it in
"The Next Wave":

> . . . though bravely through each throat
> the slogans rang . . .

they have no effect upon the feeling of waves, waves of life and the
continuing wave drawing toward death, as

> . . . we catch our children's eyes
> on us, westwardly welling with goodbyes.

Kramer, secular man though he is, does not take shelter behind
the grimly brave, bravely grim fig leaves of Hemingway or Sartre.
With proud immodesty, he bares those fears which both mas-
culine and conventional religiosity command one to cover: the
inborn fears of illness, loneliness, and death. See "Night
Thoughts," "Windchimes," "Yawn in Empty House," and "Going
In" for powerful treatments of love and death. Then see "At
Trudie's Trivia Door" for a more complex poem that unites the
terror of rape with sanctified sexuality by the agency of

> . . . some invisible judge
> who smirks somewhere.

Then too, "Without a Camera" suggests that

> . . . something more clever
> than what rules from the skull
> decided

to spare Kramer from tokens of loss and separation.
Finally, in "One Year the Leaves Were Late," out of a flippant
but sinister introduction, horror emerges

[23]

> when winds nailed hail
> against my wall

marking his home for doom,

> . . . but thankgod the door held shut.

Here, we come full circle. The seeming orthographic evasion, "thankgod," unlike the "hell" mentioned above, fully achieves its expressive purpose. Here, the modern, Western infidel ends, and the timeless skeptic, citizen of the world, has his beginning.

1 February 1990

Indigo and Other Poems

INDIGO

Maybe there is, after all,
something behind it—
something that summons me
out of a deepening blue
and chooses me to choose
not the "wingding climax"
of a '59 thriller,
but JAPAN'S LIVING TREASURES:
the grower of dreamwild paper,
the potter afire with his kiln,
the poet of pleasurable dolls,
the sire of ninety-six bells
each with its soul, its cry,
the prince of Kabuki,
sixty-eight, at the mirror,
who makes himself maiden.

Then suddenly
(maybe there is, after all,
something behind it)
she, nearing ninety, I
nearing sixty, the age of her daughter,
lean toward each other:
she unmindful of lensman, I of screen.

One more thaw, alone, she has sown it;
one more fall she forces her bones to earth,

pulls back the bedding of straw:
yes, it is waking;
though daughter may lend a hand,
great-grandson be led, be shown,
Mrs. Chiga it is
who, hunchbacked, bends to the making.

Now four great indigo spindles,
her harvest, her doom,
rage blue in her nightly sleeps, only hers;
day after day at four she stirs;
with dawn's first ray she leaps at the loom;
fingers of parchment, shuttle of rust,
old mates, they know the way,
but always the thrust, the throb is new,
once more a begetting, once more a breed of blue.

Now four generations, she leading,
flow to the river; the blue is rinsed,
it will live a hundred years, will deep and deep.

Then suddenly
(there is something)
I am told:
"Mrs. Chiga died on March 28th."

For the death of a stranger, ninety years old,
I need not weep;
as for the indigo rows, she sowed them in time;
they have bloomed, been reaped;
the loom is not widowed; it knows,
they know, the way: one lent a hand,
one looked, all flowed to the river;
but oh (I pray) the blue rage
that summoned her day after day before day—
let it be mine again, not ever to lose!
mine, oh you something!
why else would you choose me to choose?

THE NEW HOME

What he has in his hand are papers:
contract, mortgage, survey—
over and over he studies
the street name, the footage,
the monthly carrying charges.

What he has on his tongue are plans:
storm windows, cesspools,
a finished basement—
over and over he speaks
caresses to the body of his house.

What he has in his skull are hopes:
unmeasured, uncertified,
unfiled in duplicate at the county clerk's office,
wild hopes
that maybe here the sun
with a somewhat sharper touch
will conjure green shoots out of him,
that the moon may slip its madness
in through these uncalked frames
in to his slackening cells.

He should drive past
over and over
and look at it squarely
so as not to hate it afterward

for being—instead of a witch's hut
in an 80 × 150 circle—
merely a three-bedroom house with carport,
in which he is destined to doze
night after night
over astounding news bulletins.

Visitors

It's come to this: set in from the window
so that when they arrive
they will not see him straining his neck
for the sight of something alive—

he studies the carpet frenziedly vacuumed,
the coffee table ranged
with Anatolian coasters and trays
for visitors long estranged

who'll feed him bits about far-fetched cousins
of whom he need not know
and yet of whom he'll inquire more
when they finally rise to go

amazed and charmed to have found him so gracious
but less amazed than he
who just last week pronounced them dead
now teasing them back for tea.

Fire

Day broke half an hour early,
and from the south.
He pulled the curtains back:
a small frame house;
from floor to floor,
wing to wing,
flame ran high.
In moved the firemen,
set up a ladder,
squatted on the roof,
hacked it open,
entered through a window,
stayed a long time,
then handed something out.

All this he announced to his wife
and they conjectured grimly.
His eyes, however,
were fixed
not on the dying walls
but on the living gold
that rose from them
like a laugh, a bride's hair,
a torch
about to be snatched up
by some new runner
headed home
with golden tidings
from Marathon.

Quarrel

If any voices could unsay "Let there be light!"
I thought those voices surely could and would that night,
could uncreate the very walls and floors and sons
they'd given shape to, years before, in softer tones.

Since we, beyond their sphere of power, felt overpowered
by such titanic rage, how must the boys have cowered
as, wave by awesome wave, that unparental thunder
crashed down and tore the tender frames of them asunder!

Morning. The sun steps forth, at once resumes command,
surveys our trouble-maker street: unwounded stand
the houses; not one bough is split apart, not one
just-opening petal of one lilac-ear undone.

The boys emerge: hair brushed, shirts buttoned to the rim.
Apparently, not the slightest loss to life or limb
has after all been suffered. Summoned, both go running
—and off they ride. For all my craving, all my cunning,

I cannot, through their windshield, fathom the expression
on either principal in last night's wrecking session,
by which to guess whatever else may have occurred
after sleep took me in the middle of a word,

or where the car is heading now: to church? the bay?
an aunt with whom the boys have been assigned to stay?
Sharing such night, such day, such blooms, it seems unfair
that what their resolution was I'm not to share.

Neighbors

They rounded the corner out the street,
we rounded the corner in—
a perfect meeting, if one must meet:
from passenger's seat, from driver's seat
a handwave and a grin.

No need to confess they'd guessed us gone,
no need to admit we were—
if she seemed dwindled to skin and bone,
if I seemed less a man than a stone,
no need to be making a stir.

For all we knew, they were off to shop;
for all they knew, we'd just been.
Had panicky parents rung them up?
Were we with a pulse about to stop?
Their auto's simonized skin

reflected ours as ours did theirs,
then—easy as boat from boat—
four grins dissevered in equal pairs:
two rounding the corner in with cares,
two rounding the corner out.

The "Mural"

At the far corner of the pool,
as if to plough through an Olympic-size
oasis, clean and cool,
had not been Paradise
enough, they hung a "mural"—a tropic strand: one palm,
one beach chair; at the left
a water, royal blue and calm:
one fin, one sail adrift.

But these days, struggling to the pool's far end
where it is twelve feet deep,
I'm pulled from the bland sand,
the beach chair vapidly asleep,
to the sea-sixth of mural, blue and still:
it holds me, till I hold
the pool rim hard, with my last ounce of will,
while twelve feet deep burns cold.

Outside Penn Station

Even before I noted through the streams
of rain and homeward rushing forms
that crutches kept the stark black face afloat,
there was no doubt—
whatever he was waiting for,
the storm to slacken or his stamina to rise—
he surely was not waiting for a handclasp
or a kiss;
what opened to his gaze
was continents beyond the swinging doors
of the hotel across the street
and what he heard, though loud about him sang
umbrella vendors, were
voices or one voice toward which he leaned,
perhaps a whisper
vending a whole self once for his whole self.

Parking Lot

Four women walking:
three walking, one learning how—
one, to whom the others lean,
seems to be learning,
but not for the first time.
Something has made her forget.
Imagine forgetting what one has known for years!
Or maybe she is blind.
Maybe she would fall if they did not
arm her.
Four women speaking:
three speaking, one learning how.
What they say I cannot hear,
but surely it must have to do with how she walks,
for already her feet move more in step with theirs
though something still pulls her
to lie as flat amid the autos
as something upstairs she has just left behind.
What they say must surely have to do
with not lying flat amid the autos,
for now they open the doors of one,
now they drive out of the parking lot
into the traffic lights, the telephone numbers,
the sandwiches.

Scarf

A mile a minute her mouth went; but the hands
worked slowly, knowingly, on his silk scarf:
untying it, tying it better, brushing it
down, fluffing it up. Her face had been
through several wars and depressions; her hair was too
purely blonde, too large, not to have come
from a lesser department store. He, however,
was faceless. If not for the outsize plaid tweed cap,
and—back of it, pathetically curling
upward—some sticky strands, he might have been
a precociously full-grown, amazingly
tolerant son, a pup, a teddy bear
trained to stand on its hind legs, propped
against a platform pillar, in her hands.

Weeding

Although at ninety-two he still had teeth,
the walk was now a shuffle,
the talk was now of little else than Death
(his prize in the next raffle!)—

therefore she checked the odds, joined him for half
an hour of serious weeding
(his specialty)—but when she gasped "Enough!"
the same old smirk, the chiding

of fifty years before, sprang to his mouth:
"Gardener!" That word got her.
In vain her dizzying toils. He still had teeth;
he still knew how to bite her.

Job Interview

Once it began, it rolled on, easier
each minute. He would round out this one
presentation, by rote unfurl his colors,
seriously jot down key-turning names
on the back page of the brochure, and leave
his handshake for the files. This time, however,

the decision would sit lurking behind *his* smile.
This time the letter from *him* would fail to arrive.
Never again, he said to the fountain, stuffing
into a trashcan beside it, the brochure,
will you enjoy my shadow's benediction,
nor you, sky, be flattered by my thirst.

"Fine," was enough just now for his wife; no need,
no way to explain just now with how much ease
and power he gazed through the windshield, done with
    struggling
to master the layout of streets, apartment rentals.
The palms returned to being exotic; the mountains
again belonged on a memento slide.

No more inquiries at the pool as to what
these heavens might do in August. He knew something
they didn't. He'd made the decision on them.
His sky, desk, standard were eastern. Let her
swim. After the plane ride was soon enough.
Or maybe August . . . yes! definitely August.

DENTAL APPOINTMENT

1.

On Wednesday, his one free day, the arboretum
two miles off—its mallards, oaks,
ripplings—for which through fifty
city years he'd thirsted—surreptitiously
he parks away the car, sneaks in
for a ticket (the man wishes him
a happy day), in a corner prays
no one he knows is waiting for the train
whom he would have to tell it's to the city
he's heading, for a tooth that crazily
broke off one night, after the news, as he gently
bit into a Graham cracker—a Graham cracker!!—
a tooth he could just as cheaply get replaced
here in these dentist-clustering villages.

2.

Clutching a worn manila envelope
laden as usual with papers and books
he'll probably not read on the twenty-first floor
in the waiting room whose magazines are waiting,
he picks the passageway where manikins
still raise their arms in a once-stylish gesture
past Gimbel's basement toward the downtown trains.

[41]

Perhaps because he is late, the route pries on
forever, no matter how fast he moves. What stench
this morning? a paint job, slopped on ceiling and wall,
whose drippings he dodges, nearly tripping over
a pair of ancient female varicosities.
Ominous footfalls behind keep his head
half turned, and he'll have to do some fancy
stepping, avoid eye contact, when he reaches
the stationary squadron of young toughs
waiting for who knows what, not him he hopes.

Out of the walls, in mean calligraphy
toward which the paint job creeps as if afraid
of the confrontation, he is again and again
screamed at, accused, given intimate instructions.
The next smell clarifies itself: someone
has recently puked. He approaches a stereo roar
(one store still doing business! hell's office)
whose cadence joins that of an incoming train:
two enormous madmen guffawing at fragile
scurriers doomed forever in this low-roofed
murderway between two crunching walls.

And, hot as it is down here, a sudden vision
chills him, propels him forward: what if . . . what
if there's no stair at either end, no side door
into Gimbel's cheery price-tags, no
downtown train for him and his envelope
and temporary tooth? what if there's only
this, forever to hold one's breath against puke,
piss, paint, forever tripping over
varicosed legs, sidestepping ominous squadrons,
forever slashed at by unsigned messages,
forever scurrying but never outrunning
the twin guffaws, the terrible guffaws.

3.

The waiting room hurts, like certain music
too intimately reverberant with ghosts
including one's own: a green-souled aria.
Full of appointments, full of juice, of teeth;

often among his fellows a known face;
in this room, thirty years ago, at each
announcement of his name, vibrations woke.
Below, in Union Square, dramas unfolded,
contrapuntal choruses raged—the lyrics
ever urgent, the last note unresolved,
but for him it had been resolved, and he gazed down:
tomorrow's emperor of all he beheld.
Dreams in regiments poured roaring fists
anthem-high into the hug of this Square
which as generously now as to that passion
gives herself to a sole hot-dog vendor.

4.

Your ache lifts to the twenty-first floor,
dips back in the adjustable chair,
and at command your adjustable mouth
opens wider, wider, wider
until the clock on the Con Ed tower
leans in like a confessor's voice
or like the eye of God Himself
watching for the scream to come,
wondering why it does not come,
prying the central shaft of your mind,
reaching the inmost vein of your soul,
telling you: Child, it's half past four.

5.

Twenty minutes before the gates open.
Surrounded by strictly forbidden soda
fountains and carcinogenic hot dogs
and phones which one by one an aging
gentleman explores for dimes,
he chooses by habit the nearest booth,
shuts himself in, and faces the dial.

Two million local numbers await him,
a life waged in this town! But the ache
that gave him notice back in the tunnel

[43]

persists; it comes back, breath by breath,
not huge, but he feels it would climb to the tip
of whichever finger dialed a number.
His mouth has been wide enough for one day.

Seven minutes before the gates open.
He lugs himself onto a bench, and grimly
examines (once an uplifting, favorite
pastime) faces of sisters, of brothers
—no longer with awe, but at least with compassion:
never, please, never with contempt!
The gates roll open; the ache is aboard.

6.

What was it? the rush for a door that anyhow shut in his face?
the burger, only half down while halfway down the street?
the crackle of brain against brain, swordplay of smile against
     smile?
Whatever it was, it has nested in the left room of his chest,
and nothing can budge it—antacid, nor shifting of tilt, nor
     breathing
as deeply as one dares without engaging it,
nor dozing off (he remembers a man who died on a train).

Billboards bleed into each other: a candidate's smirk . . . a play
they'd liked . . . a restaurant they'd been to (disappointing) . . .
Not only the landscape darkens. At least the lights of the town
come prettily on, not his. All he's not been, not done
shrills past; had he the power, the calm to seek out pencil,
paper, there isn't a proverb, a phrase, that comes to mind
for a mourning child to find among his effects and clasp.

Numbly he drives from the station, eats a few mouthfuls numbly,
numbly puts on pajamas; but the pillow he fights, afraid of
finishing while asleep—unsummarized and vague.
At three in the morning, either the call of bladder or Montauk
Express awakes him; the pain has dwindled; his wife's breathing,
the touch of her toe, flow like a drink; he has after all
not died; there is the need to attend to, then sleep, then
     morning.

"Cheerleader Killed; 'Best Student' Seized"

(New York Post, 25 January 1982)

Nothing startles me except the fact
that I'm not startled. He did act
quite unrehearsed:
amid the rest he burst
in and, coincidentally,
sat himself next to me,
at once engrossed
in just those pages of the *Post*
which, unintentionally, throughout the trip, he's thrust
under my nose, as if to cry: You must
put on your glasses; there's good stuff
here!—But the headline, the two photos, are enough.

I seem to have known a long while
their official seven-dollar studio smile
under this headline would appear
next to me on some lap, some train, some year.

Passengers

With every subtlest quaking of the car
we subtly quake;
on both of us the same sunbeam
lays its blessing;
we are
as good as twins—except that I'm awake
and mad with guessing
at the smile
that hovers and alights and passes, while
you dream.

Reflections

Manufacturers Hanover windows modernly slant.
As the express rams Hicksville, never slowing,
a pair of legs, reflected in some panes,
hurry a torso to the train after.
Optic drollery! just what photographers look for . . .
But I am neither the glass of a Nikon lens
nor of a bank that passionlessly takes
a pair of legs and coldly lets them go.
Outside the range of panes a hurrier's eyes
for three seconds follow a train's reflection
ramming west to the city with me, with me.

Platform

Approaching Jamaica with split-second speed, you will miss,
if lucky, a putrid erosion, the prop of a nightmare
that ought to be glanced at and fiercely forgotten in fog
or in rain or in moonless midnight, but never as now
in the sun's merciless sampling, where not one
freight car lugging its freightlessness to the yards
has dared to stop, to slow, even for a blizzard,
in fifteen years, in twenty; where not one rat
bothers to ferret out the last vile crumb
from one last donut gnawed at by one last
three-piece lordling large with attache case;
where not one vandal in seven years, in twelve,
has blared his name in place of the sign that once
declared: MY NAME IS . . . ; now, for some unnameable
sin, left nameless to the slow jaws of seasons
that take whatever is given them and chew it
but would, if permitted, puke up this loaf of hell.

Object Seen from Moving Window

Lit by sun and eye both in an instant,
and marble-white as an artifact of Troy,
amazed, amazing amid tracks and wires
—a toilet seat, fine-carved.

I wince when the washroom door on a train swings open.
Worse at night, in the blare of store-front neons:
their centerpiece, their prize, an imperial throne
awaiting its manikin prince.

But in Sunnyside Yard? unable to hide as a sail
on a sea, no privacy for its ghosts, not a shred,
nor for me—to whom its contours are familiar
and warm as the palm of my hand . . .

Eva!

Way past New Haven, three miles to Branford
(so says the billboard, but who's ever heard of Branford?)
a whitewashed wall redly addresses
all trains: *I love you, Eva!*

How dare you, careful calligrapher, confess
such a thing, as if I could leap from the car
and match you with something equally pure: *I hate you, Roger!*

How old are you? and she? how long ago
did your fact become true? is it true yet? is it love
of body or soul? did it burst forth not to her face
but to a whitewashed wall she daily passes?
How dare you embarrass the Line, and me in particular:
shouting what ought to be whispered into one ear!

Brazen, brazen! yet after such fields and inlets
it is your voice only that follows me east.
Brazen, brazen! yet, give me paint and brush,
I would not for any dollars white you out,
though you chose a wall, a plain white wall, for the red
burst that should come the instant you yourself
and Eva come: *I love you, Eva!*

Local

East of Jamaica on the Montauk Line
the lawns grow fresher, the air grows fine,
the cheeks grow fairer, the school tax fails,
and a lad from the ward lies down on the rails.

Southshore Line

Since anguish railroads down your spine
and eyelids scarcely open,
why have you purchased one more time
a ticket for the Southshore Line
that used to carry hope in?

There's not a pair of New York eyes,
even where crowds flow densely,
in which your own would recognize
the pure bright outburst of surprise
that pleased you once immensely.

The swans of Babylon, from whom
you seek a serious answer,
turn their stained backs; in New York's noon
each truck, each bus replies in fume
from backsides stained by cancer.

Why give your body to a train
so comfortless, so costly?
Why must the ghost of you again,
after so many miles, remain
unpassengerly ghostly?

Could you decipher the response
to all the why's that grind you
of New York's buses, Babylon's
blond fleet of uncommitted swans—
you'd put these trains behind you.

But having staggered home without
the hope unhoped, unspoken,
next week, next month, you'll buy, no doubt,
another ticket, and set out
once more with lids half-open.

Tie-Up

Lugging home through the underground
the dangerous new address of a daughter
where silences crouch for an unarmed sound
and ducts drip blood disguised as water

there is something to be said for a train
that suddenly turns from tiger to turtle,
then, with one long screech of pain,
dies in its tracks near Columbus Circle.

Motorman, conductor on the intercom
misconceive each other's question;
a mouth you could fist begins to hum;
five minutes more—you'll miss your connection;

your pressure rides to a record high;
then a lurch, a roll—a hard-won rescue!
Half through the terminal you fly.
The rail doors grin—it was all to test you.

And for it all there is something to be said.
Your imagination, overactive,
with one long screech of pain went dead—
you see now from a fresh perspective

your daughter's dangerous address,
the monster maybes that await her
in the lobby, on the ledge, in the wilderness
of a loafing eye, on the elevator.

MIDNIGHT IN OAKDALE

Rounding the thigh of my street, I move
lawn by lawn, slow as the moon's touch
and inexcusably tender,
up toward my driveway.
No child of mine ripened here,
and of those I waved to
the last is away at college.
A new batch dreams of December,
of snowballs and my windshield;
their parents have made the connection
between me and my unkempt forsythia.
Slow as the moon's touch, inexcusably tender,
I move—dwelling by dwelling—
toward the one whose basement cracks
widen
still damp with last week's rains.

At Night

All at once the dogs set up a racket
and I know that something's in the street
prowling at the garbage
stirring up the pebbles
fumbling at a lock.

Not a light goes on. Are all the houses
out cold as she is, she beside me
lips unlocked
fingers half unfisted
drawing darkness in like ether through the nostrils
letting a deep dream out?

Suddenly a tread rounds the corner
a tide closes in
a claw pulls down planets
things land, take up position
radios crackle
searchlights violate hedges.

And the street offers nothing in resistance
nothing but this innocuous breathing
and the toothless racket of the dogs.

Night Thoughts

"Died in his sleep . . . so lucky!"—How do you know?
You had no attack last year, nor afterward
with friends sat mute, death-still; yet even you
have lain for hours counting your dearest in coffins,
imagining them and finally you among them,
your name above-ground gradually fading
to less than the whisper a branch outside your wall
will send somebody else not caring whether
that somebody has an ear as loving as yours.
For hours you've lain without an eyelid stirring,
so as not to disturb your wife, and if she does
wake for a moment, how could she know that you
are anything but asleep? and how could his wife,
who knows more than the rest of us put together,
know he was lucky, know he died in his sleep?

Windchimes

There's nothing else to hear at 2 A.M.
while sipping warm milk than the chimes.
At Greenport Fair we purchased them
in our first rural times.

For years, with cousins found at other fairs,
some outworn, others still unwrapped,
they woke when we came down the stairs
and when we slept they slept.

April, and two young sassy squirrels grew;
our gable seemed to suit them fine
no matter how the westwind blew
to make our scarethings chime.

But 2 A.M. is an unlucky hour
for human residents who rove
beyond their bedroom's sphere of power
to a chime-haunted stove.

The milk which desperate for sleep I warmed
warm as a lullabying breast,
suddenly freezes, is transformed
to ice cubes in my chest.

Old Tunes

Last year, when he noticed a pain in the pit of his stomach
as soon as the Beethoven *Seventh,* or *Egmont,* came on
(the things he'd conducted alone as a boy in his hammock
with ever-diminishing carrot or pretzel baton),

how simple to switch off the set, give a twist to the dial . . .
but now comes the cricket chorale that was once his delight,
the wave, once so lilting, the wrath of the wind, once so royal
—no switching off these; at their mercy he quails in the night.

Nightsongs

1.

If only one day cool and light I could step out of bed,
leave all of it fevered away, sweated out on the sheet,
no trace of it crouched in my bones, in my veins, in my head,
and merge once again with the cool and the light of the street!

This happened—I heard years ago—to a friend of a friend;
besides, I remember a book about just such a case;
and once, when I woke, it did seem to have come to an end:
I thought I was shaving the last of it clean off my face.

2.

Patient as the parent of a slow-learning child
the rain, since eight last evening, has repeated it
in the same slow, expressionless tone, on every
inch of wall and roof and dream, and even now
at three in the morning,

with scarcely half a wisp of reprimand
begging me to listen just a bit harder,
implying some reward if finally
I say it too, say it and understand it,
while there's still time.

3.

What of the anniversaries unmarked
in your most private calendar
that crouch in ambush till the dead of dark,
then jump out at your jugular?

Hero

To tear his head from the chair
was a decision:
leaving behind
a glob of blood and hair.

The TV switch
clicked off.

At the crossroads
he veered
from the heated blanket,
marched head high
to the front,
slid aside a drape
and stood his ground, though wincing,
under the fire of the stars.

DIALOG

(4 July 1976)

Here comes that migraine, otherwise known as the Muse
of Politics, whose Greek name I have forgotten.
More and more forced, more and more unpleasant
her entry, and always with the reminder that once
I summoned her, opened a window for her
to tear the tongue from my throat and replace it with fire.

"Yes, and instead of falling asleep at the fire,
tonight of all nights, you need me," mutters the Muse.
"America's having her birthday—look at her
pulling out of the closet all her forgotten
costumes of freedom and kindness that suited once
when serfs adored her and despots found her unpleasant!

"Who if not you," she cries, "will proclaim unpleasant
tidings? The hearts of your countrymen are on fire
with hate for the poorest, which they themselves were once;
abroad, leagued with murderer kings, they amuse
their mother goose skulls with imperial games;—forgotten,
America's pangs, when empire pounded her!"

Two aspirins give me courage; I answer her:
"Old Muse—old friend—if what I say is unpleasant,
forgive me. It's touching, not to have been forgotten
by you, at least. The veins I set afire

[63]

long since ran cold, and mine await a Muse
of milder aspect than they welcomed once.

"Somehow the tidings that could rouse me once
from a young wife, the waiting lips of her,
no longer turn me. Soberly I muse
on shames as deep, days no less unpleasant:
Garrison mobbed, the Pequod tents on fire
—wickedness heaped on wickedness, forgotten.

"Find someone new; you cannot have forgotten
the way it happens: he'll welcome you at once;
his window gapes; already he's half fire;
his wife calls gently, but he sidetracks her;
and if she's jealous, things will grow unpleasant;
small wonder, being jilted for a Muse!

"Go tell him, Muse, America's forgotten
glories! Let his unpleasant rhymes that once
roared through my jaws, set her again afire!"

In the Fortieth Presidency

1. In Wicked Times

It is, after all, my planet.
My father trained me to care.
Night after night at eleven
I've somehow managed to bear
shipwrecks, planewrecks, dreamwrecks
—with ice at the roots of my hair.

Once or twice per decade,
for several months in a row,
the times were more wicked than even
a trained man cares to know.
Those nights I moved toward the dial
with footsteps chill and slow.

For several weeks I've noticed,
just about half past ten,
a frost in the pit of the stomach,
a craving to flee the den;
I crawl to the dial—no question:
the times are wicked again.

2. On Entering My Home with the *New York Times*

To carry such things home is a disgrace!
As if I were a carrier of the plague,
each plant, each drape, each painting in the place
palls at the page 1 face
of Haig.

3. All-Star Neutron Day, 9 August 1981

(On the morning of the annual all-star baseball game, the president announces
full production of neutron weapons. The Asian sonnet form was chosen to
commemorate the destruction of Nagasaki on 9 August 1945)

The mouths of Auschwitz's unholy pillars
sent sacrificial incense toward the skies.
Now men ask: From the womb of Bachs and Schillers
how could there be a leaping forth of killers
without one gasp, one turning down of eyes?

At 7:30, just as we were drinking
our orange juice, the pillar of the land
that was the womb of Whitman and Abe Lincoln
sent from his mouth a smoke. Men will be thinking:
With gasp, with lowered eyes, did no one stand?

Here's how it was: twelve hours went past; the smoke
had settled in all lungs; we settled too
and switched our tubes on; pandemonium broke
in Cleveland's ballpark—red and white and blue.

4. Bhopal

There is a wailing in my skull.
Until I set it free,
my nation's poison ravaging Bhopal
will ravage me.

Each artery of mine, each vein
from forehead down to feet
is thronged with mourning, thunderstruck by pain
—a Bhopal street.

Two thousand ghosts in pantomime
beseech one word of blame.
Until I find a name to fit the crime,
it has my name.

5. Bitburg

Why suddenly astounded
does the planet gape
as if a new voice had sounded,
a new form taken shape?

Was he so much subtler
that you could be beguiled?
Long since in deep hell Hitler
guessed what he was and smiled.

Why should he not bring honors
for the brownshirt dead?
Look at his living gunners!
Listen to their tread!

Those killers, could he wake them
after forty years,
would leap wherever he'd take them
with bayonets and cheers.

6. Rendezvous in Hell

There is in hell one cranny set apart for those
whose regiments were claws that clutched at all the planet
and whose police were fangs that pierced the throats of foes.
Come, muse of Dante, for without your flame I cannot
unfold that scene! Surrounded by the damned in chains,
their sentence is to be infernally at leisure,
to smile in dreams of empire over lush domains
then start up and behold the ashes of their treasure.

7. Honduras, 18 March 1988

Behind the smooth cosmetic smile,
behind the glib softspoken guile,
impatient crouched the killer frown
—now it comes parachuting down.

No longer need I ponder why
it has not been my doom to die

like grandfather, at twenty-four,
uncle, who ailed seven years more,

father, expelled at fifty-three.
A nobler span was granted me
so that for each new show of force
I still can bellow forth a curse.

Be my countrymen quick or slow
to hear it, let the record show
that once more in a wicked time
at least this poet raged in rhyme.

Street Scene

These out-of-businesses
eight on one street
catch at us
as if we owned shares in them
or stored prime memories of them—
first grownup haircut,
first trousers, let out slightly in the seat—
or had a stake
in the town's future;
but no,
we merely pass them hurtling east
as we zoom west—
can't even say
what town it is—
eight storefronts:
bankrupt, broken, boarded up.

News Item

Into a corner of my skull
there dropped a word.
Plague? Impossible!
Absurd!

I clipped a second nail. But yes!
again that sound.
Plague! a seventh case
tracked down:

fever . . . cold sweat . . . a coughing fierce
and uncontrolled.
Plague! In through my ears
it rolled.

New Mexico . . . the stricken mother
is Navajo.
Plague? I trimmed the other
big toe.

AIR FOR BAGPIPE

Behold the success of Burns' style!
In through the tourist turnstile
year after year come spilling
thruppence, sixpence, and shilling,
all for sight of a letter
written by Burns as a debtor
begging that death might come
not in jail but at home.

The Masters of Düsseldorf

(The professors vote 44–41 not to rename their university after Heine,
Düsseldorf's native son)

With so many poets large and small,
what need was there for his birth at all?
And if it was destined to come, what pity
not to have scourged some other city!
And why not a century later? Book
and body together would rise in smoke.

The Yucca

"Read not the Times. Read the Eternities."—Thoreau

Halfway down the street in early July
on my way to the *Times*, I stopped at a yucca as though
entranced by its clamber of frail white cups, and so
I was; but Thoreau held my inner eye:

not he, freer in '46 behind
bars than his townsfolk reveling outside;
not he, when John Brown mortally was tried,
who climbed his town hall steeple and defined

Manhood and Life and Death; but he who could
(according to report) have been set down
blindfolded in a forest miles from town
and after weeks allowed to see the wood.

Studying lights and shades, studying flowers
and shrubs, he would have known the hour, the day,
reckoned the distance and shown the shortest way
to Concord. These, more than his moral powers,

held me. That day I brought back to my rooms
more than the *Times*. I know when the yucca blooms.

Legacy

Whatever else happens to you and me,
if all goes well, you'll sit on my knee,
girl, two years from now, or three,

just as, embarrassed, I was won
by Ella Reeve Bloor in '31.
She pulled me to her and said, "Son,

"in Camden that's the way I sat
on Whitman's knee—yes, just like that.
'Ella,' he'd say, 'let's have a chat.

"'Did you know that in Brooklyn, when I was not yet
six years old, and a teacher's pet,
I was lifted and kissed by Lafayette?!'"

Charlie

This afternoon, in fog and rain, we drove
twelve miles, and for a somewhat bloated price
beheld a somewhat bloated film, and strove
to be entranced, but dozed off once or twice
Dinner was midway over when we came
to mention it, and fumbled for the name.

Fresh-minted after seventy years, tonight
across the television screen, in black
and white, once more there sauntered into sight,
wielding his cane, moustache, wide eyes and hat,
the little fellow with the outturned feet
marching toward the Goliath of our street.

Alfred Kreymborg's Coat

We shared initials and a passion for reform.
High in his Charles Street flat I drank my first martinis
and floated home.
Soon he signed his letters "Uncle Alfred"
and at sixty-five declared me his inheritor.
Three times my age, he poured into me what was his:
where I now sat, Sandburg and Crane had sat.

At last, while loving him, I marked those pourings
as lessons of how not to be if by some miracle
I lived past sixty.
One night he phoned, announced "a storm of poems!"
To me, whose years were then all storm,
his exultation at the floodgift was as strange
as the long drought preceding it.

Later his wife described how every morning
he shuffled to the typewriter
and sat there
as if the old keys might revive
what had so many years commanded them,
then mournfully arose, the cold machine
once more betrayed by, traitor to, his fingers.

Afterward we drove to Stamford one last time.
A ritual was called for: Dorothy must give me
some part of my "uncle."
I would have settled gladly for a snapshot,
a manuscript, maybe a first edition.
But she'd determined otherwise: an overcoat,
well made, not often worn, was my inheritance.

How could my face show anything but gratitude?
The sleeves, I lied, would instantly be shortened.
I never put my arms through.
My son-in-law was just the size: it solved
his shiverings awhile, then probably descended
to one of his impoverished younger brothers
if not into thin air together with that marriage.

Sixty-five now, it's not his coat I walk in, but his shoes,
pouring into poets not one-third my age accounts of
the great ones in my life,
but not yet willing to sit through a morning
with fingers motionless over my typewriter,
not settling yet for the betrayal of its keys
as my inheritance.

Press Interview

Preparing to embark
on his Italian death,
reporters queried Pound;
but not a single breath
was he about to waste
beyond one crisp remark:
"My tongue finds, after sound,
silence more to its taste."

Centennial: "Live from the Met"

(Marilyn Horne sings; Bidu Sayao listens)

The curtains part. Set back behind the microphone
and lighting focused on one trill alone,
sixteen sopranos: a December tree
of faded divas, each a tunereft bird,
sit in unsocial insecurity;
but one leans forward into every word.

> *Tell me that you are returning to your Dalila . . .*
> *Repeat the loving vows you made so long ago . . .*

Wasn't it enough that hand
and face and voice collapsed,
but must you set me here now in the eye of all the land
for seven minutes, trapped
as if until the end of time
by her full-throated, her full-chested prime?

> *Respond to my tenderness . . .*
> *So does my heart tremble waiting for your voice*
> *to comfort me . . .*

The rows, a Samson ravished by my long caress,
now with no memory of me at all
except a name brushed past at intermission
under that excruciating photo on that wall,
or—if some do recall
their youthful passion
for my Dalila—wondering was the cheer
deserved, considering the seduction
they now hear

[79]

and in a little while,
after the breath
returns to their taut bodies,
will praise in thunder;
till even I begin to wonder,
I who once held Gaza with my guile,
now barely able to keep undisclosed
what huddles
behind my artfully composed
unenvying smile.

The arrow is swift to carry death . . .

For Benjamin Moloise, Hanged in Pretoria Prison

(18 October 1985, 7 A.M.)

1. To Myself

If, knowing he'll be hanged tomorrow,
you nonetheless enjoy a full night's sleep,
implying that your sorrow,
though real, is not particularly deep,

there's no need to barrage your ribs with shame:
except that both of you are human
and each holds high a rebel poet's name,
what else have you in common?

Wide as two hemispheres, two oceans,
the gulf between you: wide as black from white,
wide as a slave's emotions
from yours, whose acreage laves you with delight,

wide as the farewell greeting guards forbade
her fiery firstborn, from your mother's
embrace of you: a gray, grandfather lad.
—Sleep well; you are not brothers.

2. The Ballad of Mamike Moloise

At four he whispered her to wake,
but she was up and dressed.
They did not sob, they did not speak,
they somberly embraced.

[81]

She passed the dreamers in their beds
and murmured: "Since my son
gave voice to what was in your heads,
why should I walk alone?"

At five the sun screamed forth his rays,
and unto him she called:
"You're right to set the sky acraze
who were my son's true gold."

A bird went by on wistful wing:
"Fly to Pretoria jail!
Since you first taught my son to sing,
now sing him a farewell!"

And to herself she spoke: "Because
the daybreak drove him wild,
and his the wingéd creature's laws,
I called him Special Child.

"Am I to blame because he saw
with what a pride I smiled?
Should I have taught Pretoria's law
instead, to such a child?

"Instead of wings, instead of dawn,
should I have suckled him
on ordinary milk alone?
am I therefore to blame?"

At six her shadow fell outside
Pretoria's prison door.
The whipmen and their bloodhounds cried:
"You'll see your son no more."

"I have no fear of jaws," she said,
"I have no fear of whips.
Just let me press, before he's dead,
my lips upon his lips."

At seven each ray of sun became
red as a poet's blood;

[82]

and wide as a young poet's dream
the wings of birds out-spread.

The dreamers of his dream uprose
and roared across the Square,
embracing her with daybreak eyes,
with cries that winged the air.

3. To the White Minority of South Africa

Open the Book of Time, if you have eyes;
turn to your page, and know it.
The State that slays its poet swiftly dies,
but never dies the poet.

THE TOURIST

sits forward
rather than back
gaping left
gaping right
so as not to miss
a remarkable tower
or gulch
amazed
that some town
never heard of
unfolds
street by street
traffic posts
firmly implanted
women
in kerchiefs
responsibly striding
as if expected

The Word

In the Neretva Valley, not far from Jablanica,
halted by rockslides, we remembered
our kilo of cherries, and held them out
to a truckdriver, who said "Hvala!"
—For a handful of Mostar cherries
we learned our first and last Croatian word
Hvala!
Cool and green, like the Neretva.

It was not much, but enough
for the service-station attendant at Ilidza
who put down his lunch, wiped his face
behind a little curtain, came out
and drew an intricate map of where we must drive;
the tram conductor in Zagreb
who instructed the man to put the boy on his lap
so one of us could sit;
the pharmacy clerks in Ljubljana
who held a grave consultation
because from the looks of me it was clear
I needed more than a gargle.
—Hvala!

At the very last, rounding the mountains
between Ljubljana and the border,
when suddenly the skies gave forth
on pines, barns, steeples, and our little Fiat
a single eloquence,
instead of cringing at the hammerdrops
I answered Hvala! Hvala!

O Minos! O Rhadamanthys!

Last night, after Knossos, after a swim
    off the cool stones of Aghios Nikolaos,
suddenly I stood witness at a wedding of strangers.
The crowd was as gay as old; love-crowns tenderly lifted
    onto the bridal heads;
I just saw the pair's drawn, a little frightened faces;
the double kiss of family members;
wristband for him, neckband for her—
(you can find their names on the register of St. Titus Church).

Tonight, after Phaestos, after a swim
    off the hot sands of Matala,
suddenly I stood witness at a maiming of strangers.
The crowd was as somber as young; stretcher tenderly lifted
    into the ambulance;
I just saw his length of dark hair, bandaged face twisted
    sideways;
one told me he was a famed singer, cut by a windshield;
the dead, an old woman, had stepped in front of his taxi—
(you can find their names on the register of St. George's Clinic).

O Minos! O Rhadamanthys!

Rhodos

One of Ulysses' lands you surely were, Rhodos,
so close to Troy—but which? of Circe, or the lotos?
Maybe the lotos; flowers were everywhere,
insinuating fragrances along the air.

How long, winning isle, till I be won?
Loll! you hissed—and loll I might have done
to the last drachma; so the Norsemen did,
on cots disarmed, under umbrellas hid;
their smiles were of the lotos plant,
though none grew drugged enough to chant
We shall no longer roam;
—after the one-week package deal,
on Monday morning they'd be home
watching the suntan peel.

Now . . . as to Circe: though the Norsemen drank and ate
heartily, loud and late,
one ought not call that turning into swine:
the alcohol content in Retsina wine
is barely 10 percent;
if there were loftier things to do, they might
—yet few blonde heads appeared at night
in Old Town for a "Cultural Event."

If there was any serious turning into swine,
it was on one of Rhodos's most Class A streets,
right at the Lindos busstop, where the line
became a mauling, shoving, cursing lunge for seats
—to reach Athena's shrine!

If there was an unquestionable turning into swine,
it was the waiters, taxi drivers, vendors

who saw us not as pilgrims treading without sound
Greek ground
having since childhood memorized its splendors
but as rich food
to be chewed
and spewed.

One of Ulysses' lands you certainly
were (or both . . . as isles and mainlands tend to be);
I might never have escaped alive
via Olympic Airways, had the Number Five
—the bus seductively marked PARADISE—
(it was, no doubt, a destined hour;
it will, perhaps, not happen twice)
not whizzed right past
so fast
jammed to the door,
I wonder yet what look the riders wore,
unto what sty or bower
they might arrive.

Mycenae: On Brushing One's Shoes in Athens

So: as I feared, she finally did speak
about my shoes; and actually I must
brush off these particles before they crust
as particles will do in one dry week.

But not so easily from off my cheek
shall vanish the descendant of the gust
that brought Mycenae tidings of Troy's lust
for Helen. On his tower I stood, his shriek

came at me from that bathing room; I trust
that war, that homecoming; and—though I seek
no quarrel with my wife, having grown meek—
my dust has mixed with Agamemnon's dust.

Madrid: July 1978

All day I staggered about, unable to shake off those three
visions of Goya: the white-bloused Palace defender, arms wide,
   about
to join his comrades heaped under conqueror bayonets;
the Infant Time beheaded by his Father's teeth; the things of
   night
leering their black mass of triumph . . .

All day I staggered about, unable to shake off the posters
summoning Spain's "New Force" into Madrid,
into the bullring wide as Saturn's jaws
to tear at the frail new day, to hymn July 18th: when bayonets
pointed at the north, the Palace.

Now, back in bed, I am reached
by a rumbling from a region, of a kind, unknown.
You might call it the whir of nightlife traffic;
for me it is once more the insurgent artillery
closing in on the city . . .

But a loudspeaker reaches me too—enflamed, enflaming—
protesting yesterday's army attack on Pamplona,
passionate as that which bloomed through the last nights in '39,
saying there's sap in it yet; after thirty-nine years
it could bloom again!

And I, who came to salute ghosts, salute Time instead:
Saturn's new child, unawed by his brothers' fate.
If, as the grafitti around the corner threatens,
the army will strike again, the "Fuerza Nueva," rumbling
even now into Madrid

[91]

in caravans of cars trailing red and gold streamers,
black-massing even now in the bullring, tucking chains
and batons into their trousers along with what's already
there risen and ready, Time's new city
will not lie back and take it.

Barcelona: The Last Night

I am lying past midnight
thinking not of a woman but of a city.
I have always been susceptible to cities—not all:
some I hate outright: the arrogant ones,
the ones who want my money,
the man-eating ones—
from them it is bliss to escape!
some I both hate and love,
including the one that cradled me;
of those I love
I touch not a hair
—they never suspect I am there.

It is not blind love, Barcelona.
I took note of the driver
who doubled my fare,
the guard at the beach gate
who denied me a glimpse of the sea.

But inside the cathedral a Sunday handful responded
in sweet Catalan (forty years outlawed)
to the priest's chant;
while out in the square, hands linked,
defying a hostile high noon,
four rings of gentle sardañas
revived with each cool flow
from the gaily umbrella'd musicians;
and the side-street one-man show:
juggling oranges four at a time,
blowing Ping-Pongs ten feet high
and homing them in his mouth like doves,
coaxing frail melodies
from Catalan veins around him,

catching them one by one in his trumpet
and blaring them back full-fledged
into the veins that had nested them;
and the multicolored cartoons
turning old walls into young screams for freedom;
and the lad in the bookstore, the crone at the hotel,
eyes flashing, back stiffening:
"Of course I am Catalan!"

Granada: First Showing

No, we did not join the pilgrims
plodding heavenward (by taxi)
to the caves of Sacromonte.

No, we crossed the street for tickets
and in sweltering Granada's
lobby, pressed by youthful speech and
flesh, grew faint, before at last the
doors creaked open, and a Spanish
Gary Cooper, Ingrid Bergman
mimicked forth in large, dynamic
motions what had truly happened
eight kilometers from where we
sat, up there in the Sierras
forty years ago, which parents
could not murmur, poets would not
sing, remembering foolhardy
Federico's riddled body.

Better than the best flamenco
to be found on Sacromonte
was the silence of Granada
rising row by row and bearing
home the shriek of Ingrid Bergman.

Córdoba

No sulking terminal weak in light but powerful in urine,
no dragging of luggage up long shadeless ways,
no disappearance of passports—
no! Straight from the bus one should enter the Sultan's gardens
out of whose shrubs the sweets of de Falla pour;
deep in the Mosque, that awesome confection of marble,
around its striped pillars,
should creep like rays through a many-mythed window
the most reaching notes of *Iberia* . . .

My Córdoba neither sang nor danced.
Outside El Corte Ingles, in Saturday brilliance,
a blind girl chanted lottery tickets.
Outside my meditation
the synagogue caretaker paced his toothless craving for lunch.
Inside Isabel's most forbidden of nooks,
around her decaying bathtub,
a gang of guttural wisecracks splashed like mud.

On the second and final day
the museum was locked but the fountain ran free in the plaza;
the market sprawled dead,
but the balconies laughed geraniums;
on the inside lane of my nerves a midnight scooter braked,
but a girl hopped on
and off they zoomed inventing a breeze.

So up to the sixteenth-story roof I came
to give Córdoba one last chance.
There below in the darkness floated her lights.
Without strain I lifted them into me, one and all,
along with an illegal pup and its walker
I had suddenly embarrassed near the ledge.

The Voice of San Miguel

After the Honda roars its last turn
then perhaps to you
for whom Valium does not work
comes the wild footfall of one Otomi
unseized by
the conquering Aztec
who in turn fades frowning
into the Hills of Moctezuma
as white legions psalm past
spew prayer execrations
—death-cries of dissidents
teaching the rest
to kneel at last before the Cross—
now an invasion
patio by patio
bill of sale by bill of sale
subtler sounds, a clink of tequila
haggling in quaint shops
over serapes and tin masks
exasperated gaspings
across rabid rivers
that were docile streets
till a frown like a cloud
from the Hills of Moctezuma
chased you all the way back
to your Castilian toilet
to wring out victimized stockings
and curse the day you picked Mexico
—Mexico!
where Valium cannot quiet
the calves of your legs
or keep from you
after the Honda's last roar
the voice of San Miguel

Learning by Stages

On Sunday, while his would-be luncheon host
muttered somewhere, a painter sat engrossed
in muraling our skulls with current life:
the sexes more at peace, the racial strife
settled. "You know, in Cuba's every vein
Africa dances—Africa and Spain."
"What of the Indians?" "No—not a trace
of them; they proved a proud, unsmiling race.
Rather than kiss the Cross, they chose to leap
as one, into the mercy of the deep."

Days set. We'd nestled at a beach hotel.
Wresting myself one midnight from the spell
of disco drum, deep chair and shallow speech,
I crossed a road, a pine woods. At the beach
the sea suddenly rose, gnashing its teeth
—bright heaven above it, black hell underneath.
At once I shook; either its primal roar
had seized me, or a vision: This the shore?
these stars? these woods the tribe had bid farewell?
given its heart here to the ocean's swell?

We're at the airport, on the customs line.
I draw Estella's body close to mine.
Her lips are Cuba. In her eyes the cape
of Hemingway she'd led me to takes shape.
I ask its name. She tells me: "Cojimar."
Why Coji? One last patient smile: "There are
legends . . . old local legends . . . From this spot
they say the Indians leaped, preferring not
to live in chains." Without a word I turn
and take through customs what I came to learn.

[98]

Flood

". . . nature hath shouldered Cornwall into the farthest part of the realm, and
. . . besieged it with the ocean . . . a demi-island in an island . . ."
—Richard Carew, *The Survey of Cornwall*, 1602

"The Lionesse was destroyed on 11 November
1099," the *Chronicle* sobs: a region
wondrously fertile, inhabited by a race
of comely people,

builders of gleaming cities, a hundred forty
dream-high churches whose bells in the clear of summer,
in the blue, in the rock of waves, can still be heard
gently tolling.

Once, as Lyonesse slept, the riled Atlantic
lifted a vengeful fist and, flooding over
all but her highest peaks, engulfed the towns
in swift succession.

On a still night—Mount's Bay fishermen tell you—
house roofs can be seen beneath the water.
On a June day, at low tide, you may glimpse
the ghost of a forest.

At neap tide it is possible to gather
beechnuts, and cut wood from trees embedded
in sand. At Trewa, tin-stream works decay,
older that Cornwall.

Each year at springtide's lowest ebb the children
of all Perranuthnoe, in hope of finding
treasure, flock to the sand 'round Cudden Point
(some are rewarded).

[99]

Into this parish, aided by the swiftness
of his white horse, before the wall of water
Trelawney (or Trevelyan) fled—they two
alone surviving.

And what of Lelant? Aye—and what of Phillack?
Were not they meadowland? Were they not smothered
by sand in one night? Were the ancient towns
not somewhere seaward

of the Black Rock? Was not old Lelant churchyard
washed away? Are human teeth not sometimes
discovered even now, after a great
undertow scratches?

Night floods Newquay (new in 1640!)—
Newquay, with its famished high tides daily
munching on beaches, eyeing this hotel
for a real dinner.

Night floods Newquay, and I clutch the bed frame
so as not to be washed away, as the old harbor—
somewhere seaward of these toffee shops
and tour charts—vanished

one night . . . or century . . . away with the bustling
mines, market towns, pilchard vessels,
crosses, customs, words for hello, goodbye,
a washed away Cornwall.

ANNIVERSARY WALTZ

Though obviously I approve you,
it wouldn't do well to seem rash;
so for thirty-eight years I gave you
each Friday a nosegay of cash,
and even shaved off the moustache
—but never allowed that I love you,
nor thanked you for doing my wash.

The Slippers

Dragging my slippers from their hiding place
was invariably hailed
by the remark
that even in his bedroom after dark
for a man in my position
to put them on was a disgrace.

Considering their condition,
she was right: their backs flopped open,
innards trailed
like the pitiful wake of a pair of broken
boats
or the echoes of two failed
trumpet notes.

She soon confronted me
with mounds of slippers, 8½ E.
But, despite their elegant design,
somehow one and all
were either loose behind or small
in front: I saw my future on the refund line.

Of course the time I knew must come, arrived.
The pair predestined for my feet connived
to find me; still, I wore
my five-year ruins five years more
on special mornings, when I woke unwived.

Words

Having said too much, they now say nothing.
It is a marvel that the living room walls
are smooth, the pictures all hang straight,
the lights work. At least one slingshot,
had her brow not stopped it, surely would
have gone through the window; and if not
for his receiving groin, a tomahawk
must have split the Steinway in two.

Having said too much, they now say nothing.
Corbies should be circling the chan-
delier: peering down, counting.
It is quiet as a field of battle
after loud carnage: the last two arrows
have found each other's eye; a red
gurgling from gullet, chest, and thigh
has won the interest of vermin.

Having said too much, they now say nothing.
Withdrawn behind magazines, they quiver
with words inflicted and taken, as if
destined to resonate until
the head on the coffee table opens
its lips, or the cactus prophesies,
or the oil burner—whose stable voice
they never craved before—goes on.

Tree

She had taken a dislike to it; that's all.
She had other plans for the space it occupied.
It wouldn't've helped one bit had the creature cried
(as maybe it did): "Remember, before my fall,
how long it took for me to become this tall!"
She said it was blighted, said the sap had dried,
said in a storm one night it would crash inside
the careful architecture of his skull.

Suddenly there hacked a crew of four
—while she, assured her orders were understood,
businesslike went in to start the meal.
It took them over an hour to split the core.
It took all winter to turn the limbs into wood.
Now birds in the boughless air bewildered wheel.

Reunion

She allowed my invitation;
he allowed her to accept—
on the usual condition,
which, as usual, we kept:

not one session at the piano
with a tune they both dislike;
not one word about the clan who
flourished forty-five years back;

not one replay of a picnic
we'd been privileged to attend;
not one fumbling for some knickknack
reminiscent of a friend.

At Trudie's Trivia Door

Although at first you feel
it was unfair
that some invisible judge
who smirks somewhere
should sentence you without appeal
to face a windshield smudge
outside the door
of Trudie's Trivia, on a backstreet in Bay Shore,
and though at first
you wonder for what crime
you have been cursed
to sit here marking time
while she considers knickknacks for a friend
whose party you would rather not attend,
suddenly—whether blinking
has cleared your sight
or shifting from left butt to right
has cleared your thinking—
the scene is not as worthless as at first:
although this day
was meant for monitoring sunset from a pier
at Great South Bay
not half a mile away,
still you can see and almost hear
the bay breeze nudge
a drowsy maple's bough;
three broken windowpanes
over the bridal shop
are blazing; now
they stop;
one stubborn spark remains
on the roof's top;
and now the gloom

downstairs that must all afternoon
have waited for its cue
steps through
the storefront glass and like no tender groom
assaults the bride
on tremulous display
who, even if she tried
to scream, could not escape
her nightly rape—
for not a single human shape
in half an hour has passed
and the proprietor
when he comes forth at last
does nothing more
than roll a lid of metal down
as if she's guilty of the unsold gown.

All at once
the door comes open; stair by murderous stair
your wife grimaces, grunts;
the very sunray from the bridal roof
consoles her hair
and kindles in your groin a proof
if proof were needed there
that it was neither worthless nor unfair
to put you on a backstreet of Bay Shore
at Trudie's Trivia door.

Lip on Lip

All night around their house
the crazy winds carouse;
with interwoven arms
to keep them from such harms
they count the groans of boughs

till in a partnership
of rolling thigh and hip
they pull the electric blanket
over their heads and thank it
humbly, lip on lip.

Yawn in Empty House

At one bound
the great yawn leapt
from bed to hallway, loped
without hysteria
the length of it, and crept
through kitchen, foyer, dining area
seeming to look,
but neither hoped
to find nor found
in any nook
an interest in sound.

He takes the path his yawn took; all
answer with silence: paintings down the hall,
her cup there on its hook,
her saucer in the rack, half-dried;
the window-drape
through which can vaguely be descried
the driveway and her auto's absent shape.

He turns the radio on, then off:
no need now for a lush
romantic tune. Rid of Rachmaninoff
the hush
grows doubly deep.

At last too from his innermost cave escape
the questions: What if no yawn had made the leap
this morning—but a sigh
in need of prompt, compassionate reply?
—a gasp, a clutching at the chest
that calls for tender language, loosened tie,
ambulance and the rest?

What if it found,
room after room, such total lack
of interest in sound
—not only with a new day's light
but late at night
when every car but hers that should be back
was in its driveway, every head of hair
but hers that should be just above its quilt, was there?

HOW CALIFORNIA WAS

When you asked how California was, perhaps
you saw me almost separate my lips
to bore you—like those ever-ready chaps
who probably keep entries on their trips—
with tales of reawakened fellowships,
kissing games, word games, coffee spilled on laps.

There came a night: somehow our lungless friend
managed a word; but his bed-engine's pulse
gave me to hear, from the land's other end,
our grandchild's unborn heart. Now home, I bend
to catch that embryo tune; but something else,
a gasp, comes at me from across the land.

Grandmother

Smiling she sinks back into a vision: tomorrow,
through tunnel and over bridge, she will fly
to where he dreams now, knowing nothing of it,
and will know nothing of who she is when he wakes
and finds her hand reaching the milk to his mouth,
her eyes reaching the sparkle to his eyes,
her lips reaching the love to his belly button.

But the smile fades: this is his final dream
of knowing nothing, the final dream from which
he'll wake knowing nothing of who she is
when he finds her hand reaching the milk to his mouth.

The Cliché

I'd coursed through seven counties
of green and gold and blue,
eyes fixed on the macadam
whose every inch I knew,
while flocks around me flew.

We'd just swung off Route 80
onto the Garden State
when a breeze reached in through the window
invisibly as Fate
and made my brain vibrate.

I blush to confess the vibration
—it was just an anemic cliché.
By the skin of my teeth I triumphed
over my naïveté
and managed not to say
"How pleasant it is today!"

Perhaps it was that my nostrils
had cleared in honor May;
perhaps it was for our daughter
and hers, twelve miles away;
I don't remember the visit
except there was food and play,
but I do remember the wonder
and—even more—the dismay.

My wonder itself was the wonder:
whose edict do I obey
these thirty years, forbidding
the pulse to go astray?

There are some alive who remember
it was not always this way.
A thousand times at the Bay,
Fort Hamilton to Sea Gate,
in weathers glowing or gray
forehead fronting the spray—
a thousand times on the railroad,
clay against sweaty clay—
a thousand times on pavement
without one golden ray—
I dared to think, yes, whisper:
"How pleasant it is today!"

Grins

Just on the verge of widening her yawn
to bellow for a breakfast bowl of dawn,
she all at once recalled who lay in bed
across the hall, and nibblingly instead
knuckled our door. Big Sister dared to knob.
Once I was theirs, Grandmother knew her job:
out came the Kodak, freezing into place
forever, grinning face on face on face.

It ought to be among my favorite prints,
but never has escaped the drawer. I wince—
as at a mirror—every time I dare
to sneak a look. It isn't that my hair
juts wild and thin, or that I'm in the same
pajamas their own mother, when she came
marauding in on Sundays, brushed against;
it's that I'd never previously sensed
the holocaust of my ungoggled eyes.

Well, neither looking glass nor Kodak lies.
As for the girls, if rather than a lens
we'd faced a looking glass, that pair of grins
sandwiching mine would not at all have faded.
My lips, not theirs, would curl the nether way.
I did not know my face as well as they did.
—Perhaps I'll come to love the print some day.
Clearly, as far as those two were concerned,
what mattered was the grin toward which theirs turned.

[115]

Greg Norman's Five-Wood

First: the man teeing off was not
O'Meara or somebody close behind him
but Norman, no better than minus one,
to whom I'd never paid much attention
nor would have then at the fifteenth hole
had the commentator not happened to wonder
why on earth he'd chosen a five-wood
(until he swung it).

               Second: my wife
crawlingly brailled her way back into
the chair; but though it was a recliner
she leaned far forward, keeningly silent,
pillowing her head on her knees.

Third: in the corner next to the double-
door I can't yet bear to blot out
with drapes, though all beyond is sunless,
greenless, sits the tiny seat
that along with its half-chewed crayon box,
its wild-hued papers, should have returned
to its roost behind the basement stair
as soon as I'd returned from waving
goodbye to our daughter's militant bumper.

And now Greg Norman swings; four hundred
feet the ball rides, like some flying
saucer in from outer space,
making clear to the commentator
(but not to one shocked, dispossessed
Monterey gull) why he'd chosen a five-wood,
landing plunk in the middle of
the green, a zoom lens scooping up

three bronzed, plump Pacific grins
in sportswear, blimp shots suddenly pouring
all of it into the gray of our den.

And I beg my wife to take one swig of it,
all that vitamin-D-packed midday
green of the Pebble Beach we'd passed
heading south in '63,
she at the wheel, who now, to be civil,
glances neutrally at the screen
and nods and lowers her lids again.

And as Greg Norman confidently
marches past the cheering toward
his second swing, I march as well
to the abandoned corner, wish
for a five-wood, but lift instead
the little plastic seat at which
an hour ago the girls, as always,
wrote "tickets," sending us this time
to Zambia, Spain . . . apparently
as unconcerned with what's to come
at them as that Monterey gull (before
Greg Norman's singing thing soared past).

Granddaughters

1.

To have them both! not trapped inside a frame
seeming to smile at me each time I pass,
or—at third hand—reports of cleverness,
of soccer prowess, but the actual *them!*
—one at each side of me, on a park bench
facing the Hudson!
                    Obviously I lost
control, and turning to the younger, pressed
her less forbidding hand, as during lunch,
and whispered: "Nice scene?" How could I have guessed
that even she, at nine, would answer: "Boring"?
The pilot polishing his prow, the ripple
sporting in sun, the stream of healthwalk people,
and I, the actual I, were far outclassed
by last week's crime show, yesterday's wild scoring.

2.

They're such sophisticates, such heavyweight
scrappers now! and I'm
so tired . . . !—They've outgrown walking on my feet
just in time.

Time Machine

After the rolling up of one of the rugs—
the one from the den—
after the last of the picture takings and hugs—
for one more grin

I was inspired to turn my final chore
into a caper,
bestowing upon the garbage a cylinder
of toilet paper.

Then they were off: three heads of long black hair,
she at the wheel,
they waving. Later, in the bare
den, my automobile

brain was suddenly on the move; it sped—
a time machine—
not west to Jersey but fifty years ahead
to a family scene.

Something—perhaps the reminiscent cleft
in a grandson's chin—
will set one of my granddaughters adrift:
she'll be again

in Oakdale, in 1989, and he—
alert, asquint—
will see them in the car waving at me
as off they went,

I in the driveway raising with a roar
the empty roll:
"I lift my lamp beside the golden door!"
And he, all smile,

[119]

—miming "Give me your tired, your poor!"—may lift
past five decades
his clasp toward me, my clowning prop, my cleft
among the shades.

EPISODE

1.

Tomorrow morning
at nine-fifteen
I'll have my turn
at the truth machine.

Backhead, forehead,
left side, right—
much will be clear
that is vague tonight.

While I and some others
lie awake
wondering what
reports it will make,

it sleeps in its freshly
patented youth
ready to graph
tomorrow's truth

at forty-five-minute
intervals—
be it death, be it life
that dens in our skulls.

2.

Right now in every corner of the planet
one by one the billions are falling asleep
hungry or full, in hate, in love, in trouble;
even, at last, the ones who meant to keep
vigil all night beside the wife, the husband
assigned tomorrow afternoon at three
for more sophisticated tests and X-rays
because today's were not as they should be.
        Later, somehow
        even those
        drop into calmness
        and their eyes close.

3.

Although the news brought no upheaval,
no silences, no tears,
at night she laid upon his navel
her hand, more dangerous to evil
than radium or prayers.

Before the gesture could begin its
withdrawal, over hers
he placed his own right hand, and in its
hush, for their marriage's best minutes
the pair held intercourse.

4.

So, one more mystery's solved, it seems,
for me and the handful I choose to share.
For you it remains as dark as the dreams
and lusts and what else walks everywhere
under my clothes, my smile, and my hair.

The death now locked in my cage of bones
you soon will see as my body's cage.
One mystery yet: will I beat with moans
at the bars? fall brooding? blaze into rage?
or, shrunk like the sibyl, at last turn sage?

5.

Since I was just the least bit frightened,
the skies have only somewhat lightened;
the breeze-inspired birches dance
with scarcely more exuberance.

In fact, the sun now seems less able
to praise the food upon my table
than yesterday with its fond touch
when I was frightened, though not much.

In the Suburbs

District by district, borough by borough
left behind
till not one year, one street remained
free of sorrow.

Fifty-five miles beyond the last pavement
of that town
he found a lawn on which had grown
no bereavement.

After one year he hadn't stopped smiling;
after five,
he passed the chair in which sat Dave
greening, paling.

After the seventh, he set the loud table
at which Death
fed silently; after the eighth,
he switched trouble

on, where the lamp grinned Marian's laughter;
after nine,
he put a disc of darkness on;
yes—and after

ten, with a thirst that leaves him aquiver,
he'll await
the phone voice that he used to hate—
hushed forever.

How many years are people to wander,
and how far,
before they're free? Past what grim door
must they blunder?

Nick

At night, in a blizzard,
for the first time in twenty-one years
the face of a yard worker comes back
—round, grimy, one tooth gone—
and his first name, Nick, and his husky laugh,
and that long, tough family name
I lettered on his envelope each Friday:
G E R O L I M A T O S . . .
Nick, youngest of the crew.

When he took sick (having worked outdoors
through a blizzard, thinking his hulk would protect him),
what a surprise, bringing him his pay,
to discover two grown children
—the boy a math whiz, wilting under his praise,
the girl coaxable to the piano—
both blonde and goggled as their mother
who kept them and her apartment as immaculate
as he was smudged with grease, but not that day.
How clean he lay, laughing in bed!
How clean, one month later, when we put him in the ground.

Several Miles Apart

At seven this morning, several miles apart
on the same south shore, two poets are pulling clothes
mechanically over groin and heart.
Had the second not by accident heard news
of the first, he might check the length of nail on his toes,
of hair in his nostrils, give ear to the weather report
while downing cereal, and as the coffee brews,
gape at the ice-gripped car with a prayer it will start.
And though he knows that the other, the first one, hurt
beyond all howling, probably will excuse
himself from the breakfast table with a short
whisper just about now, and though he knows,
having his own, what it must be like to lose
one's thin, blonde twelve-year-old, one's devil, one's squirt,
three hours hence forever to the rows
of rock, and in a rain, who used to dart
at whim past the solemnities of art,
cavorting through Mazzaro's, Ignatow's
cadences;—still, the mind turns to a shirt
proper for mass, a proper word to use.

On the Death of Someone Else's Grandchild

And so the phone call ended; there was time
for others on the list, but they could wait.
Coffee as well would have involved the crime
of opening one's mouth; best face the gate,
and when it opened, trudge inside the train
and through a sooty window watch the sky's
appropriate grayness drop appropriate rain
to reprimand the dryness of one's eyes.
This left an hour and a half or more
out of whose hush a requiem might be wrung
before one reached his depot, then his door,
with a bizarre contagion on the tongue.

[127]

The Death of a Friend

Two weeks have passed since the first call came;
how then can it be to blame?
Nor did it come from him to me,
but from wife to wife in secrecy:
no longer would he go to his job,
nor Fridays to his district club,
nor to the window for sun or moon,
nor open a paper, nor lift a spoon,
nor, when she spoke, admit he heard,
nor open his mouth to let out a word.

Ten days have passed since the worst call came;
how then can it be to blame?
Besides, no germs had been involved;
they'd had a problem—now it was solved.
It wasn't a case of conventional ills,
but merely a matter of seventeen pills.
Besides, it had nothing to do with me:
our date was for seven; he did it at three.

The box was closed by the time we came;
how then can it be to blame?
I did shake hands with each of his sons,
did kiss his wife and his daughter once;
—perhaps from their eyes I should have hid:
eyes that, before the glossy lid
was lowered, had looked their longest and last,
and into mine their look had passed.

A week ago last night we came
back from the wake. Is that to blame?
Is that why my thoughts are astir with contagion,
symptoms, period of incubation?

Early this morning I became
aware of something, something to blame.
It's not that I'm medically ill,
but merely a matter of lacking the will
to look at the window or even the wall,
to march my body the length of the hall,
to hear my wife, to lift my head,
to open my mouth for a bite of bread.

The Face of Rose

In that split second between sending silent thanks
for getting through the Midtown Tunnel in one piece
and throwing my nervous system to the doggish ranks
down Second Avenue, there's suddenly the face
of Rose; it's merely one of those mysterious pranks
played by my mind or on my mind these days.

That split second is always hers no matter how often,
reaching the intersection, I make myself remember
she's not on the twelfth floor uptown, but in a coffin,
and nothing good would come of dialing her number,
which sometimes I did dial, did sometimes set her laughing
with flimsy jokes, but not since last November.

She'd have been ready, at the undropped drop of a hat,
arrhythmia or no, to leap south on two buses
even if only for a measly half-hour chat,
to fondle with her voice our undeserving voices,
which we begrudged her, I keep mumbling with regret,
as we begrudged her fondling face our faces.

I have no doubt, although the image that reappears
is always kindly, that it calls for retribution.
Already I foresee the sentence of the years:
some face, some voice we would have leaped to with devotion,
having got through a tunnel, poised for thoroughfares,
grant one split second at an intersection.

Reunion

As Claire flew up from Florida,
her message flew to me:
this time I was the nephew
she needed most to see.

While I was putting on my tie
and brushing back my hair,
"I wish I knew," my wife said,
"the magic of Aunt Claire."

About ten miles into the trip
I passed my father's plot
and yelled "I'm seeing your sister!"
—whether he heard or not.

I cupped her shrunken form in mine.
Could this have been the knee
on which I laughed at Chaplin
so hard it made me pee?

That peak in my biography
Aunt Claire could not recall;
as for great-aunts and -uncles,
she knew and named them all:

where each had lived, how each had died,
and who'd belonged to whom,
she rattled off. Her phantoms
soon overran the room.

Lighter by twenty tons, Aunt Claire
went home the way she came;
and so did I, my riders
loaded by date and name.

Toward the End

1.

My uncle, at eighty-nine,
smiles and insists he's fine,
believes his daughter's his mother,
greets his son as his brother,
sings nursery songs in Russian,
engages us in discussion
concerning some boyhood foe
whose name he expects us to know:
some rascally trick that's been done
to him and his brother/son . . .
and he tells it in such a way
as if it had happened today.

We come away from him crying,
convinced that his mind is dying,
that his thoughts are disconnected,
his lost streets resurrected.
At first we hoped he was joking,
but he smiles—and the mattress is soaking;
he dozes—he visits the grocer,
the cobbler; he's coming closer,
half waking, half in a slumber,
to a birthday, his third December,
to his father, who last night beat him,
to his mother, who soon will greet him.

2.

Till now the problem's been
his drifting out of days;
now it's his drifting in,
tongue still fiercely ablaze
(though he can't dress himself):
Where is she? gabbing again?
And where is the crowded shelf
that comforts now and then
with its knickknacks and photographs?

This time, at the blaze of his tongue,
a male alongside laughs
and back to his bed are flung
in twos and tens the curses.
He calls her name, he calls
for the attendants, the nurses;
but those he knows, like the walls,
are on another floor.

He is about to doubt
the omnipotence of his shout,
but a face appears at the door—
resembles her more and more—
and he goes drifting out.

The Son

How lucky, that last hour, to be so peeved
because she only with reluctance kept
the smock, waved off a cactus she'd received,
and couldn't be persuaded to accept
the radio. How lucky, though bereaved,
though slowly from her sight he turned and crept
lifeward, to feel so savagely aggrieved
by her that final hour he scarcely wept.

Desolate, she forbade all visitors;
quaking, refused a blanket for the chills;
insomniac, would not consider pills.
How lucky to pass so bitter through those doors
he need not fly back for one last embrace
and find her hands stifling a sob-wrenched face.

Learning

It's been a long time since the last this-piece-
might-interest-you clipping:
blood-pressure pills, good posture, an increase
in hometown crime, the stripping

of forests . . . Still unwillingly, I learn
from you, though you no longer
care what I know. For instance, I discern
that being truer, stronger

than most, well paired for sixty-seven years,
won't spare one an invasion
of solitariness at last, a fierce
absence of conversation;

that all one's postmarked lifesavings of love,
one's Kodak proofs of laughter,
the furnishings one was so proud to have,
will drop in price hereafter

and soon no trace of them be anywhere
and not a soul remember
the marvelous occasions in one's care
before the wakeless slumber.

But this is old news—like the rise in crime,
good posture, pills for pressure;
why do I feel, then, that I must make time
to memorize this lecture?

[135]

The Little Swiss Sheepgirl

Unable to hold it in one minute more,
forbiddenly I hasten, pass in hand,
not to the bathroom but the assembly door
through whose high pane I see you boldly stand
there on midstage, past rows on darkened rows
of sixth-grade heads: ablaze in Switzerland!

Ablaze, the gold braids Mamma wove this morning,
the bodice she's been witchcrafting all week;
ablaze, the lines I learned as you were learning,
which all the world but me now hears you speak.
You gesture, not toward me, but toward the snows
closer by far, the snows on that far peak.

* * *

Once again I'm in the corridor;
but this time at the bathroom door I turn—
eyes shut, so that as brightly as before,
past rows on rows of darkening sixth grades,
your shepherdess's morning braids will burn,
that magic bodice and those love-twined braids!

Once again, no matter how I yearn
to hear the sweet lines not one listener knows
better than I, a sudden voice upbraids
me: "What are you doing here? Get back to class!
Her snow's Sierra, not the Matterhorn.
She's seventy—and you, boy, where's your pass?"

Interview

Two years ago (or three . . . the new times blur)
some girl—everyone's baby-sitter—came
acrumbing at our door, meek as a sparrow.
An interview she wanted! they were "at"
the Great Depression in her class, and we,
the oldest on the street, would be most likely
to have the story straight.
               Whether she used
the part about my father crawling shamefaced
home with his one or two tie-selling dollars
on lucky days, the part about my mother's
diet of stale bread dunked in deep black cups
of coffee, I wonder; but the interview
ended at that point—children have big mouths—
the man was crying, the street's oldest man.

The Next Wave

No matter how skilled the whisperings, the lies,
by twelve a child was able to figure out
the system: how it works, what it's about.
First, for example, past the western skies
great-uncles, -aunts, with whom had come to house
our future parents, teeners off the boat,
floated; next, though bravely from each throat
the slogans rang, though unscored were the brows
of father, mother—as if immortals—clearly
they were the long wave scheduled to crest;
already crested;—no matter how sincerely
we clutched at them, already headed west.
Now all at once we catch our children's eyes
on us, westwardly welling with goodbyes.

What Comes Home

The lips that kissed or cursed, the hands that bloodied
or blessed, those we can box, from those we can drive
away. As for the rest, the disembodied,
that comes home with us, *that* is alive.
The walk possesses our shoes, the talk possesses
our tongue, the smile nests in our eyes, at night
we are touched handlessly by caresses
and lipless kisses on our lips alight.

What else? Were you left recipe books? a kit
of tools? a hundred thousand in bonds or stocks?
I inherited songs—more than could fit
into the shelter of the strong pine box
where limbs rest roomily—and barbs of wit
beyond the knock of worms, the need for locks.

Without a Camera

An oversight?
It slipped your mind?
—To leave the camera behind
on such a flight!

Not to bring home the face
of a new grandniece
and of a mother you perhaps won't see
again, near ninety-three!

No—something more clever
than what rules from the skull
decided those two beautiful
faces should not burn forever

in your wallet, on your wall,
down your ever-deepening past:
one for the first time pressed,
one for the last.

GOING IN

1.

I guess it was the cornflowers' undiminished gaiety,
the squirrel's last-minute escape route up his usual tree,
the bark once more withheld in recognition of my tread
that turned my head.

In any case, a crazy image caught me as my hand
caught at the knob: that she'd be at the sink, that she could stand
without her cane and, as I entered, offer me her face
with the old grace.

2.

The building itself and its people
were new; the machine
onto which they strapped her
was such as we'd never seen;

nor had she ever been slid so,
body and head,
into a space that imaged
every bone she had.

Never had such a rattling
pounded our drums.

[141]

As for the costs, they shortly
reached unparalleled sums.

Only the days of leaning
toward a mute phone
were not new, nights of guessing
what must at last be known.

3.

"What's the prognosis?" we asked.
"Guarded."
—Four words, as if recorded
and desked.

Not unbearably painful
at first;
played back tonight, through our worst
rainfall.

4.

Gradually I drifted
from nightmare into fact.
Darkness, eyelids lifted.
She was going in; she was packed.

Neither smiling nor somber
my face confronted a face,
which, pillowed safe in slumber,
still occupied its place.

Trout Quintet

Reading was what she preferred
to the fool's look on his face,
each fumbling for a word;
and so he left the place.

Since there was only one
where recently rode two,
switching the radio on
seemed the right thing to do.

At once the *Trout Quintet*
struck at him like lightning.
Till then he never yet
had felt such sweetness frightening.

His right hand, in whose touch
her ghost of hair lay soft,
was of a mind to switch
the jet of music off.

But being at the wheel
it recognized the danger
of veering one's automobile
into a blameless stranger.

He could not, though he tried,
forgive the flow of that sweetness
—poor Schubert, who had died
at half *his* age and completeness!

Now incomplete, unnerved,
in a car without its soul,
a moment more—he'd have swerved
eternally out of control.

[143]

But Something sympathetic
—observing his pallor, his sweat—
dispensed a grace of static
against the *Trout Quintet.*

Wave after wave it came,
like thunder, like thundering hoof,
and his right hand, without shame,
switched poor Schubert off.

Homecoming

1.

Leaving your wife in traction
alone on a hospital bed
you could have come on the highway
but took the streets instead
although the traffic was creeping
and the lights kept turning red.

You'd hacked those streets, that traffic
a thousand times and more,
been stopped at those intersections
a thousand times before,
but this time for the first time
you neither kicked nor swore.

The truth is, you felt grateful
each time a red light shone
and ticked off two more minutes
the night you came alone
when her body lay in traction
and nobody lay at home.

2.

If it was a little face, not a flowerpot, all it could see
was darkness, then headlights turning, then the silhouette of me
fumbling, flashlight in hand, for a key,

darkness again, then the least kitchen light,
then a large shadow weaving in and out of sight,
dwindling, looming, then—once and for all—night.

[145]

Wise as this child may be, he's unlikely to have guessed
that the car and driver across the way, before coming to rest,
had been amid groans for bedpan and codeine twelve miles west,

that the house, if it could, when its kitchen light came on,
would have quaked with wonder why, instead of two treads, one
wakened its walls, instead of two voices, none.

3.

It was understandable,
all things considered,
not having paused a minute
since break of day—
transporting her,
getting her X-rayed,
absorbing what the specialist
apologized for having to say,
then the emergency room,
the wheelchair,
the corridor bed
on which she lay,
then driving home
his instructions,
too tired to stop
putting dishes away—

it was understandable
in half-light from the kitchen
and he by then
not even half open-eyed,
while readying for bed
mechanically
to place her pillow and his
side by side.
Nor was it unreasonable
at 3 A.M.
considering the dream
to which he was tied
that he should wince at the floor's creaking
and shut the bathroom door

good sense
would have left wide.

But having waked
at the toilet's flushing
to realize no one else
heard that waterfall,
having returned
to the bedroom
fully aware that no one
heard the creaking in the hall,
it was by no means understandable
that he should skirt her space
and as usual squeeze
between bed and wall;
to take so many
chill, rugless footsteps
rather than climb across her absence
made no sense at all.

Blue Square

For eighteen years on Union Boulevard
I glided east and west without regard
for this blue square marked "H" for hospital,
utterly thankless of how rich, how full
a gift
not to regard the arrow underneath
this "H" that hisses through its death's-head teeth:
Turn left.

"Visiting Hours Are Over"

1.

Go on, go home; it's okay when you cook
to cut the recipe in half.
Watch some TV; it's okay when they joke
for you to laugh.

What strikes you now as cruel could be worse,
so once more kiss her and go home.
Consider this an easy training course
for what may come.

Sleep twelve full hours; if, when you awake,
there issues a barbaric groan,
you, you alone will wonder: Did it break
from breast or bone?

2.

Now, unembarrassed, spatula in hand,
over three browning corn-fritters I stand
who three hours since believed my fate was there
fastened forever to the sickroom chair
while phrases such as "quality of life"
crisscrossed my vulturously measured wife.

3.

If I, whose bones are not about to be scanned,
refuse to consider the last of the berries and cheese,
how am I to dial her and demand
she get her breakfast down? Instead, I squeeze
my whole week's garbage into one small bag,
her last three crumpled tissues too, and tie it
as if it were the end of things, and drag
myself outdoors with it. The street is quiet,
but nothing like the quiet that awaits
my coming in: a morgue of breakfast plates.

Postoperative Care

1.

The last thing she did in the bedroom was open a drawer
all the way, so I'd know (just in case) what she carefully kept
   there—
certain life and death papers—then quietly moved past the door
without looking back, though for seventeen years she had slept
   there.

And then, in the kitchen, the last thing she did was to place
on the door of the fridge all her don'ts, which I couldn't but see
   there:
Don't leave lights on, the stove on, the sink water running (in
   case
she did return home she'd "be glad if" her "home would still be
   there").

The first thing she did, coming back, was examine each wall
inch by inch, not with eyes of a specialist trained for inspection,
but of someone who'd suddenly learned about symmetry all
that needs to be learned, about frames and their fragile
   perfection.

2.

Well, this time at least we were favored by luck;
we can get in the car
next week or next month and go off for roast duck
at Le Soir

or sit by the ocean and study the style
of a gull riding free.
At marvels so minimal others may smile,
not we.

Wives

Again that bit of groan
as if from the intestines, not the lips,
at once stitched tight:
unmanful to let all that pain ooze past!

That groan again, so close now
I awake.
—It isn't Joe in the next room,
a fluster of attendants' feet around him,
door shut, shade down the day I fetched her home.

It isn't Joe. It's she back on her pillow,
three weeks safe now, halfway plump,
letting a bit of moan out of her dream.

—Maybe his wife's awake; maybe this minute
she also thinks: It isn't Joe,
that groan, ah! from his lips
at once stitched tight, manfully and forever.

Anniversary

Today, by coincidence, we were heading west
with a pile of thrift-shop offerings. My wife
was at the wheel. "The word now is *divest*,"
she lectured me. "We've reached that time in life."

—My wife was at the wheel!! One year ago
today (though neither ventured to refer
to it) we'd headed west: slow was not slow
enough—each rattling brought a moan from her;
hell raged inside her skull; heave after heave,
all through a day, a night, she had divested
herself of life; what little was left to receive
the Emergency Room received, the specialist tested.

Hell dormant in her skull, dread in my marrow,
wordless today we passed the hospital arrow.

A NEW YEAR

Rounding one more bend in the river,
remembering rumor of shoal and shore,
half in rapture, half in terror
I feel each finger freeze at the oar.

April

And now the leaf of spring unfurls
to the least wrinkle;
from all its jags, like earring pearls,
the raindrops twinkle.

She looks us boldly in the face:
"Put on your glasses
and catch the moment of my grace
before it passes!"

Pastoral

sheep
seriously nibbling

all at once
a drained ewe
half knocked over
by the lunge of lambs

now
lofty-headed
she lets them take her

tiny tails quiver

nothing else
visible

Canadian Geese

I swung into my smartest left-right stride
and headed up the road in record time
to learn what notable or dream had died,
what neighborhood winced in the clutch of crime.

Not till their cry was almost overhead
did I give ear; not till they'd almost passed
from view did I agree to slow my tread
and grudgingly look up at them at last.

Of course it was a choral ecstasy
they had no choice but to express; what right
had I to guess their message was for me,
a group guffaw, a feather dropped in flight,

as if to say: Count us! such twenty-four
you are not likely often to behold;
are you afraid of getting to the store
five seconds late, the last grim headline sold?

One Year the Leaves Were Late

Tomorrow—May!
Green should bellow from the branches.
But maple, chestnut, dogwood, elm—
a whole nation—
cast conspiratorial glances;
tree to tree
confirms the resolution
to be dumb.
The time has come
to shake them: "How much longer can you bear
to hold a year
of greenness in?
You must be bursting!" What could it have been,
I wonder,
to make them take a measure so extreme?
Was it that night when thunder
tore me from my dream,
when winds nailed hail
against my wall,
when something huge and shivering and naked seemed about
to break my hinges—but thankgod the door held shut?

Had I Not

Had I not gone out to the mailbox,
I would not have found, writhing on its wings,
an infant sparrow,
lifted it from the oncoming mail truck
and set it—beak crying, heart convulsing—
in my cup of hands;
the cry replied to at last from a high branch;
a whole wing-broken, mother-craving essence
thrashing about, cupped in my hands,
doomed by the pitying smell of my palms
crying for rescue, heartbeat counter to mine,
its mother ready to drop a rescuing beak against my rescue—
a mercy killing against my merciful hands—
as soon as I left it emptied of cries,
wings awry in the bewildering grass.

Incident

We've scooped a home in our sunniest land
for the roots of the flaming flowers;
we've tied their stems to help them stand
through hurricane shock and showers;
a dark, strong soil—not like the sand
that allowed them at once to be ours.

No one points a finger of blame;
we tore them away from no mother;
they'd flung a solitary flame
acres from sister or brother—
nor stealthily by night we came
congratulating each other.

Yet with our prey we fled the field
as if the life were leaking
out of a slash that will not be healed,
at which all life is shrieking
till our name be cosmically revealed,
our crime eternally reeking.

I drop in high grass my dripping spade:
was it used to plant or bury?
Already the blaze appears to fade
I was so quick to miscarry.
What rune should be chanted, what circle made,
what rite extraordinary?

what rite for a burning without a name
lugged home in a whiskey carton?
All well and good if they keep their flame
and set aflame the garden;
but what . . . what if they fail?—Long shame
on earth, and then no pardon?

Morning Stroll after a Hurricane

With how contrite,
how smoothly blended overnight
a blue
this sky surveys
the aftermath of yesterday's
to-do:
a hundred-year-old oaken
neckbone broken,
a brash young Subaru
smug in its playpen, which a pliant,
                        giant spruce
belonging to some envious neighbor
and owing him a favor
for long caring
decided it was worth
utterly tearing
its splendor loose
from earth
to cross the avenue
and split the motorchild in two,
while nearby in the Mall
three regiments
of unpaned shoes
can tell us all
what it would be to lose
one's last line of defense . . .

With how deceptively naïve
a blue, the sky
expects us to believe
its protestation: "How could I,
I, without a wisp of cloud
from east to west,

[162]

without a whisper,
how could I fling a curse so loud,
bring so malevolent a fist
against a proud
century oak and swing and wring and
                    twist her
and leave her broken, leave her bowed
at last?"

Raking

If you don't think trees enjoy a
joke, to you it's paranoia.
I, however, have no doubt
that the minute I stepped out
in my woolen hat for raking
(with the pompon thing on top)
tree nudged tree till all were shaking
with a laugh they could not stop.

Three weeks they had woven carpets
matched in few Armenian markets;
and I had no time (no heart,
truly) to unweave such art.
Still, ringed round by greenlawn neighbors,
mine was "not to reason why."
Forth I sallied to my labors,
hat on head and rake on high.

Hours beneath them I bent double.
Each repaid me for my trouble
with a deft, a gentle pat,
knocking off my woolen hat.
When I looked, they seemed sincerely
innocent of conscious craft
—just as they've pretended yearly.
When I looked away, they laughed.

No harm done but to my splendid
lawnrug, now the raking's ended.
Outdoors there's a smell of storm.
I come in. The kitchen's warm.
Through the blinds I see my brittle
brothers brace themselves. I pull
one by one their stubborn little
leavings from my hat of wool.

[164]

Port Jefferson: A November Day

As if held by some foreboding, the year
has not yet taken from your forehead
its last tender touch.
Between your ribs, in thin, radiant rays,
pierces the gift.

Undaunted by the weather,
Christmas makes its move.
Fathers, more than their sons,
enjoy the ski outfit,
the schooner afloat in its bottle.

One turns, roars
through the oncoming thicket of limbs:
HOLD YOUR KITE DOWN, TIMMY!
Toting a package twice his height
Timmy, not two feet tall,
casually emerges
aware that what his father feels is in the package—
the dragon joy-paper bursting to leap—
not in the roar.

These others, so busy the length of the street,
do they sense what is finding them?
Such lifted faces!
seeds of care, of course,
under every smile, even the youngest,
but for a moment at least
the whole species gifted
with a sweetness lingeringly offered,
lingeringly savored,
as if this were humanity's last mild day
not for the year but forever.

New York Skyline in Cloud

On other days
each prince of them
has seemed to raise
his diadem
in pride and scorn
against the sky
beyond the praise
of beings born
to burrow down
and kiss the hem
of his steel gown
and swoon and die.

Now one and all
beneath the cloud
they seem less proud
nor half so tall
stripped bare and tossed
against a wall
the faint hope lost
the holocaust
about to fall.

Blizzard

It may have been the pattern of one storm,
but by the sudden unambiguous come
of it, just past a river, he felt sure
the train had crossed an arbitrary line
and there, there in that very cloud of clouds
the great throne stood from which a finger spoke
and mutely all gave heed: those at the right
—trees, houses, hillocks—wise enough to take
their sunbeam gratefully; those at the left
long since aware that but to whisper "Why?"
—no less than outright pouts of insolence—
might treble on their tops the chastisement,
which no one need remind them was their due
—this white-whipped landscape, white-bespat, beshat.

Penguintown: TV Special

Ottoman-hoofed, with a skull full of cocktail,
zoom in by day as the comical penguin
flipflops ashore and half-humanly waddles
back to his township

after lone months with uncanny precision
hailing his wife at the specified corner
where, pausing barely a moment for small talk
of their excursions,

briskly he gets to the business of beaking
stone after stone till their house is completed,
then to the nesting, the bliss of conjunction,
then to the hatching.

    Zoom in by night, with insomniac elbow
    biting the bedclothes, with winds—Jeremiahs—
    grinding their gall through the gums of your window.
    Zoom in by night as

    down on that fort, like a god out of patience,
    hammers a blizzard, while safe on the ridges
    skuas contain themselves, letting the gusts work,
    counting the perfect

    eggs pried away from those pommeled, lopsided
    pairs strewn asunder, a half-human army
    sunk under snow, their impregnable trenches
    no longer showing.

Storm

At two the storm's attack
was so malign, so deep,
a whiteness worse than black
appalled me back to sleep.

At four the things it said
provoked my spirit so,
I flung away from bed
and marched to face the snow.

All infantry but one
lay strewn about the field:
one spruce, surprising son,
though stricken, would not yield.

Before the misery
of that half-frozen shape
seeped through and into me,
I quickly dropped the drape

and turned the radio on
to hear of inches, feet,
in Pittsburgh, Washington
—not my own lawn and street;

but Schumann sang instead
till, barefoot as my spruce,
I lifted high a head
filled with defiant juice.

At six, its hundred harms
unleashed against my walls,
I woke to view the storm's
exhausted arsenals.

[169]

Birthday

Another storm-year, yet I stand unbroken;
stripped to the skeleton, but firm of root;
arms lifted wide, not whining for some token,
but poised to warble one more pæan of fruit.

WAKE

You wake in the middle of night
for what, at sixty-two,
has grown a nightly need.
Reminded of something right
you recently managed to do,
you muse: "*He'd* strut indeed . . . !"
—Imagine walking straighter
thirty-seven years later
across a freezing floor
and turning a bathroom door
as though each lift of each limb
were being directed by him
from under such drifts of snow
as those to which he was given
so many winters ago,
as though you may yet be driven
years from now to a deed
because you are his, his seed!

Index of Titles

Index of First Lines